The Warrior Sage

Life as Spirit

Phil Nuernberger, Ph.D.

YES INTERNATIONAL PUBLISHERS

•

We thank Lorraine Wells for the cover drawing
and Andy Pearson for the charts and illustrations in these pages.
•

For information and permissions address:
Yes International Publishers
1317 Summit Avenue, Saint Paul, MN 55105-2602
651-645-6808

www.yespublishers.com.

Library of Congress Cataloging-in-Publication Data

Nuernberger, Phil, 1942-
The warrior sage: life as spirit / Phil Nuernberger.
p. cm.
ISBN 978-0-936663-45-6 (pbk. : alk. paper)
1. Spiritual life. I. Title
BL624.N84 2007
204'.4—dc22

2007015542

Dedication

This book is dedicated to Bob and Betty Hoff,
the loving parents of my wife, Deborah.
They have inspired generations
with their great capacity for love
and their dedication to a spiritual life.

Acknowledgements

Books may emerge from a single mind, but they are always the outcome of many lives and influences. I am inspired first and foremost by the personal guidance of my spiritual master, His Holiness Swami Rama of the Himalayas and the tantric traditions in which he so lovingly guides me. My wife, Deborah, and my children, Santosha, Raka and Samraj provide the loving foundation for my life and my work. Co-travelers on the spiritual path of the Himalayan Sages, they are a continuing inspiration to me. There are countless others who contribute to my understanding throughout the years: friends, students and colleagues who challenge me to think clearly and deeply about matter of the mind and spirit. For all of these, I am in great debt. I only hope that this small book will inspire them to continue their support and challenges.

I want to extend special thanks to those who helped critique the book and provided both insight and clarity. Of significant help was the questioning of my son, Samraj, and my student and colleague, Bena Long. Their questions continually challenged me to unravel the complexity and details that I often tend to overlook. For their editorial help, I want to specifically thank my daughter, Santosha, Deborah Adele, and Diane Bemel. Their suggestions were helpful in adding clarity and focus to the writing. I also want to thank my close and treasured friend, Swami Jaidev Bharati (Dr. Justin O'Brien), for his foreword to the book. We have shared a life-time quest within our tantric tradition. I extend my heartfelt thanks to Anne Mercer and Amy Hawks for proofreading and helping me find the repetitions and contradictions. Finally, I want to thank the publisher, Theresa King, for her dedication to this book and the tradition out of which it arises.

Spirituality is unlimited, and no religion, philosophy, or tradition can possibly begin to encapsulate the infinite. This book is offered as a small step on the never-ending quest for the Godhead. Whatever wisdom may be found in its pages is the consequence of my tradition and my spiritual master; whatever errors there may be are my responsibility alone.

Foreword

The recent era of conquering outer space has ushered in an optimism that rallies all continents to hopes of a brighter, more humane future. In view of that promise, the enormous amounts of money—let alone the proliferation of jobs and the thousands of labor hours over the past half-century—dedicated to lifting a human being into the sky seem worth the sacrifices.

Now that we shrunk space and can soar around the heavens almost as fast as light itself, the deeper, broader questions still beckon: How has the glowing promise of unparalleled technological accomplishments truly benefited humanity? While we bask in our understanding of space travel, are we equally appreciative of other cultures here on the earth? As we revel in our technology, are we more at peace internationally? Is there less poverty, illness, and civil wars among the citizens of the Space Age? The answer is obvious.

Face to face with those worldwide concerns walks an author who turns our attention and our scientific endeavors toward another, more radical, direction. With visionary boldness, our writer poses that science does not have to halt at the Space Age. His modest proposal is to use science to take one to God, not merely theoretically, but experimentally, and definitely while we live. Not the external gods of conventionality supported by sincere belief, but rather the inner presence of the divine, disclosed by self-investigation.

Dr. Phil Nuernberger has a written a provocative book that defies the conventional theories, revered dogmas, and cultural formats regarding the human potential that are held in high regard by scientists, religionists, the business realm, and the public.

Leaving no major paradigm unexamined, Nuernberger illustrates the inadequacy of our cultural biases that have held society in its throes and provoked the social conditions that face us today, locally and internationally. He traces this deficiency to our failure in self-understanding.

Borrowing from his unusual educational background that spans decades of professional investigation and self-research, he points us to a humane vision summarized in his designation: the warrior sage.

The author invites us to reconsider the fullness of our natural legacy, leaving aside for a moment the propaganda and vested interests that influence so much of the daily expectations of people. This consideration is not meant as a weekend seminar in self-improvement, but rather a life-long journey, or, as the author states, ". . . of becoming truly human, of achieving our natural heritage: the integration and maturation of the inherent power of the body, mind, and spirit. It is about living with the practical knowledge and skill that bring contentment, joy, and wisdom."

Within these inspiring pages, Dr. Nuernberger provides an unforgettable challenge to the insecurity and skepticism of today's world. It is truly a vibrant blueprint encompassing the possibility of attaining immortality.

Swami Jaidev Bharati
(Justin O'Brien, Ph.D.)

Table of Contents

Introduction

We begin with a simple assertion: personal greatness lies at the core of our humanity. It is the expression of our spiritual-Self, the very essence of what makes us truly human. But "greatness" is a difficult word. It is often cheapened by association with what we have come to define as power, fame, and wealth. If someone has a lot of money, or has risen to a position of authority and power, we often refer to that individual as "great," yet these individuals are often failures as human beings. Power, fame, and fortune are all too often strong antidotes to personal greatness, not signs of it. For example, one of the defining qualities of true greatness is humility, and it is hard to be humble when you are famous, rich, and powerful.

True greatness is not defined by family name, the acquisition of material things, or by how many people know your name. It isn't achieved by graduating from an Ivy League University, being a member of an elite society, nor belonging to the "right social circles." Rather, greatness is defined by the character of who we are. It arises out of our humanity, the expression of the human spirit. To understand greatness, we must go to the heart of our humanity, the human spirit.

If we had to pick one defining quality of greatness, it would be the capacity to love. We are inspired by love to achieve greatness in ourselves. Great human beings are not perfect human beings, whatever perfect is supposed to mean. Every human being has frailties, but we always forgive the frailties and mistakes of those we love and who genuinely love us in return.

We can easily think of other qualities that characterize the human spirit – clarity, simplicity, creativity, compassion, wisdom, service, sacrifice, dedication – to name just a few. We experience these qualities in ourselves and in others at different times and in different intensities. At times we are more compassionate than others, at other times we are more creative, or show more wisdom, or are more willing to sacrifice. When we pause in our busy lives to thoughtfully consider what greatness is about, we really know the qualities that comprise greatness. We hear about them in our churches, temples, and mosques; we read inspirational stories about them; and we try to teach them to our children. But somehow, these qualities seldom determine our choices, actions, and thoughts. The truth is, in the pressure cooker of everyday life, most of us don't really live our greatness.

However, in times of crisis or trauma, our spirit emerges and we "rise to the occasion," forgetting petty needs and concerns. During these times, seemingly ordinary people show great courage, fortitude and adaptability. Then, as the crisis fades, we slip back into our ego-centered ways, and this greatness fades. We gradually revert to our "normal self" with all the habits – the fears, desires, petty wants, beliefs, and behaviors – that characterize our normal, ego-centered self.

But we don't lose the qualities of greatness. They continue to exist, deep within us, at the core of the human spirit. Distracted by the pressures and dramas of everyday life, and controlled by the powerful force of our habits, we often lose sight of, and ignore, the real and lasting power of the spiritual-Self that lies within. We will never be something we are not, but all too often we fall short of what we truly are. Instead of living the innate greatness of our humanity, we strive to become the most powerful, the most important, the richest, the most influential human being we can be. Rather than be guided by the inestimable power of the human spirit, we become a slave of the human ego and the belief systems that comprise and support the ego-self. When we do, "I" becomes the most important word, the most powerful of all concepts.

Nothing is more important than what "I" can do, accomplish, build, and win. After all, winning is everything, and the more powerful, important, famous, wealthy, "I" become, the more "I" win!

We find ego-centered behavior everywhere. It is the president who engages in sexual affairs and then tries to cover it up, or the congressman who does the same thing but condemns the president for doing it. It is the senator or vice-president who takes money from corporations and lets them decide energy policy. It is the CEO who sells his stock options when he knows the ship is sinking, and prevents the employees from selling their stock until after the price has completely collapsed. It is the religious leader who justifies hate and intolerance through religious beliefs. It is the local county or town supervisor who gets contracts for his friends. It is the neighbor who doesn't want any "colored" people in the neighborhood. It is the parent who must have alcohol at a party so people will attend.

We all face the age-old human problems of greed – for wealth, for power and control, for name and fame – and fear that "they" will take it from us. It is difficult enough for any of us to acknowledge and overcome these powerful dragons, but it is disaster for everyone when these dragons characterize and dominate the leader, whether that leader is in the family, the church, the community, the corporation, or the country.

Leaders emerge out of the population; they are not visited upon us from some distant galaxy, although the actions of many so-called leaders certainly make us wonder. The leadership problem we face lies within each and every one of us. Those that become leaders reflect the mentality of those who are being led. To have the very best of humanity expressed in our leadership, we must express that same humanity within ourselves.

The opportunity to influence others, to take a position of leadership, may happen at any time and any place. But it is always an opportunity of awesome responsibility, demanding awesome response ability. Yet, few of us have the knowledge and discipline to escape the clutches of egotistical needs and demands, to go beyond petty needs, fears, and desires. Consequently, it's not surprising that those we call leaders are caught by their egos. The more powerful (rich, influential, famous, skilled) a human being becomes, the more difficult it becomes to be free from the grasp of the ego, the more difficult it is for the "I" or "me" to serve others.

Difficult, but not impossible.

There is a way. And that way lies within each of us. Personal greatness is exactly that – personal. It is not in the words we say, the beliefs we expound, or the systems we support, but in the being that we are. Greatness, whether we lead or follow, comes in different styles, shapes, philosophies, and beliefs, because people come in different styles, shapes, philosophies, and beliefs. We live in different cultures, under different conditions, demands, and opportunities. But all of us, whether we lead or follow, start, remain, and end as human beings. Greatness resides in the essence of our humanity, and not in our religions, our politics, or our economic systems.

Our personality and character is a product of many influences: genetics, family, physical and social environment, culture, to name a few. The most common characteristic of humanity is its variety. But regardless of the variety of beliefs, customs, and all the other influences, we also share a profound core that shows itself in the human spirit. This shared humanity is our beginning and our end. It is here that we find the way. If we want a great family, a great community, a great nation, we must transcend petty ego needs and desires, and achieve greatness within ourselves. *The Warrior Sage* is about doing just that. The warrior sage is a skilled human being who lives in, for, and by the spirit, using the vast resources of the body, mind, and spirit to actively engage all aspects of life successfully and joyfully.

This book is not concerned with the kind of religious, political, or economic system we have: evangelism, capitalism, socialism, or any - ism. The concern is with something far more basic: our spiritual health. Nations, cultures, communities, and families are only as strong as the individuals who make them up. Religious conviction, material wealth, and military are not the source of personal strength. Our true strength rises from our spiritual core that is the essence of our humanity. Our greatness as a human being lies within the spiritual-Self. If we want to achieve personal greatness and express that greatness in all aspects of life, we must make this core spiritual reality our conscious foundation. We must become a warrior sage.

Let me be quite clear that I am not talking about religion or religious belief. Unfortunately, these often have little to do with spirituality. Nor is my purpose to tell you the Truth. That you will only find within yourself. But I do hope to inspire you, to demonstrate that there is alternative to the greed, fear, and hopelessness that is so prevalent in our culture. We can be individuals, and, consequently, a nation, that serves rather than takes, that unites rather than divides, that creates wealth, health, and well-being for all rather than just those who have power, influence, and money.

Although I begin by contrasting two powerful leaders, this is not a book on leaders. This is a book about all of us. We are all part of the problem we face, and we all have a necessary and critical role in its solution. In our democratic republic, as in every culture, we create the conditions for leaders to emerge. We are the foundation for leadership. In fact, according to the Constitution, "We the People" are the government. Elected representatives are only there to serve us. Or, at least, this was the way it was designed to be. If this sounds revolutionary, it is because we have fallen far from the ideals expressed in the Constitution by the Founding Fathers. If we do not confront our own ignorance, greed, and fears, we certainly will not choose leaders who will do so. Genuine leaders inspire us by their humanity; they cannot force us to be free from ourselves. So this book is really about you and me. It is about reaching into the spiritual-Self and using the power that resides within us. When we do this, we become individuals and leaders that truly serve humanity. We become a warrior sage.

Chapter One
Greatness and the Human Spirit

Nonviolence and truth are inseparable and presuppose one another.
There is no god higher than truth.
—Mohandas Gandhi—

The Warrior Sage is about a journey of excellence. Not the excellence of performance, getting to the top, or winning. The truth is that we quickly forget the so-called "winners" in modern culture. Try naming, for instance, the third, fourth, and fifth richest people in the world, five winners of the Miss America pageant, the quarterbacks of the winning Superbowl games from 1980-1985, or even five winners of the Nobel Prize for Literature or the Pulitzer. But you can quickly name five people who inspired you, five who you love to spend time with, and five others who taught you something valuable.

These are the people who made a positive difference in our lives. More than likely, these individuals are not famous or "important" leaders. But they stand out in our mind as leaders, as truly "human" individuals who express some of the finest of human qualities. These human qualities of excellence have little to do with material gain or achievement. Rather, they express our humanity, our ability to live a life of love, joy, and wisdom; an inspired life that inspires others.

The journey of excellence for a warrior sage is the life-long journey of becoming truly human, of achieving our natural heritage: the integration and maturation of the inherent power of the body, mind, and spirit. It is about living with the practical knowledge and skill that bring contentment, joy, and wisdom.

The great puzzle is that although we know what the finest human qualities are, and we know what we should do, we continue to do the things we know we shouldn't do, and don't even want to do. William Shakespeare's writings are eloquent statements of this chronic failure of the human condition, an enigma of brilliant knowing and despicable behavior. Most of us do not quite have the intensity or reach the heights of contradiction that Shakespeare's characters represent, but we share their folly and wisdom in small ways every day.

Ethics and values are more than words written in a religious text or exclaimed by a politician. They are the practical expression of the human spirit. Social leaders talk about values and ethics, political leaders claim to be in service to the people, and religious leaders tell us what we should do. But how many of us actually live the way we are "supposed" to live? How do we gain the courage to honestly stand for principles, the discipline to resist the enormous temptations that come with power, and the desire and willingness to serve rather than take? Those real leaders, the individuals who we remember with love and appreciation, don't talk about morals and values. They don't preach them to others. They live them.

We pay a high price when so-called "leaders" are nothing more than egomaniacs, obsessed with the expansion and the continuation of their power, position, and authority. Throughout history, human beings have supported, and suffered from, the "Divine Right of Kings," dictators, and tyrants of all kinds. After thousands of years of history, it's time to do something different. We must face the truth: if we lack spiritual depth and genuine commitment to serve humanity in the leaders we have, it means that we lack spiritual depth and genuine commitment to serve humanity in ourselves.

Because leaders emerge from the population, it is ourselves that we must examine. It is the greed and fear that live in our own hearts that must be challenged. A new paradigm must emerge if we are to free ourselves from the problems we face as individuals, as communities, and as a nation. While we must look carefully at the personal qualities of those who aspire to leadership, we must look even more carefully within our own hearts, at the personal qualities that define us as a people.

There is a growing recognition that leadership is personal, that true leaders lead by example, not through popularity polls or power. In *Leadership: The Inner Side of Greatness*, Peter Koestenbaum points out that "Leadership, however, like yoga, means taking charge of how the mind works – redirecting how you think and act. It is taking the oath of excellence." In other words, leadership requires not only self-mastery; it demands our personal best. It begins with who we are as human beings, and the quality of our humanity determines the quality of our leadership. It is here where we find the greatest achievement and the greatest failure in leadership.

At issue is not leadership style, but personal qualities. Knowing what to do is very different than knowing *how* to do. Telling someone that they must develop their emotional intelligence is not at all the same as giving them the knowledge and tools by which to accomplish this. We must create pathways for personal greatness, pathways based on the human spirit rather than the human ego. The overriding principle that must guide our effort is that great cultures arises from personal greatness, and that personal greatness arises from the limitless power and compassion of the human spirit, not the limitations, greed, and fears of the human ego.

Spirit-Centered Living vs. Ego-Centered Living

There can be little doubt that we can be driven by personal needs, desires, and fears. But we can also transform needs as we transcend fears and malevolence. There are times when we forget the wants and fears of the ego-self and become compassionate, fearless, and joyful in serving the needs of others. For those brief times we are free from the driving, almost compulsive, limitations of the ego. Our experience is always one of joy, contentment and a sense of great freedom. But unfortunately, these experiences are often all too rare, and we don't seem to know how to sustain this wonderful, loving, and free place. Often we aren't sure how we got there in the first place.

People who inspire us have found a way to make this loving and free place a life-style. They have found a way to live a life of service, joy, and contentment, even though they may be engaged in the most difficult of struggles. They stand out in life and in history as bright and shining stars, as different from the vast majority as night is to day. These individuals operate from a different perspective, one committed to the service of humanity rather than to a self-serving hunger for power, wealth, and position. They are spirit-centered rather than ego-centered, and everything they do reflects the finest qualities of humanity. They are human, and they certainly have personalities; they make mistakes, suffer disease and tragedies, and experience success and failure like all of us. But they also transcend the weaknesses and frailties of the human ego, and become models for the rest of us. They may or may not be religious, but they are resolutely spiritual.

The key lies in whether or not we have access to the spiritual core of our being and have the strength of this spiritual core guide our thoughts, speech, and actions rather than the ego. Most people think of themselves as consisting of body, mind, and spirit. It is also true that for most, the spiritual dimension remains only a fuzzy concept, consisting of unexamined and often unchallenged religious beliefs and dogmas. While we may believe we have a soul or spirit, it seems difficult to experience this dimension directly, and so it has little real impact on our personal sense of identity: how we experience ourselves, how we behave, or on what we place value and pursue.

For most, the sense of I-ness, or personal identity, is confined to the habits and patterns that make up the ego of the mind/body complex. We all have egos. The ego is a necessary function of the mind, constructing a limited center of consciousness that allows the other functions of the mind/body complex to be organized relative to a center of being. As one of the more powerful functions of the mind, the ego's task is to manage the resources of the mind/body. In doing so, it must maintain and express a consistent sense of individuality, or uniqueness, comprised of the thoughts and behaviors of the individual personality. In other words, the ego creates the "I," "me," and "mine" of everyday experience. Without this ego-self we cannot function as an individual.

For the personality to be effective, the ego must be strong and healthy, able to skillfully manage and direct the powerful inner resources of the individual personality. And there are powerful inner resources of the mind/body complex available to the ego-self that are crucial for achievement in everyday life. As we shall see later, these inner resources are the powerful tools of the warrior, and must be accessed, refined and directed if we want to engage and live in the world successfully.

As long as this ego-self is all we experience as our identity, then our life is determined by the limits of the mind/body complex. We then define ourselves by the qualities, traits and characteristics of our personality (such as our likes and dislikes, our strengths and weaknesses), our profession or work, gender, family roles, citizenship, group membership, even status in the community; and/or by the things we "own" – the power, the status, and the material wealth we acquire. We experience life and ourselves as entirely separate from others. We engage life exclusively from this ego-centric perspective, and our personal, individual qualities are the foundation for personal power and fulfillment. For those who have weak egos, life becomes a constant struggle to maintain some semblance of happiness and satisfaction.

But the ego isn't our only resource for identity. The spiritual dimension underlies everything we do, whether or not we are aware of it. Even though it may remain vague and undeveloped, it is the source of the love, compassion, and freedom that we experience. Through spiritual disciplines, this vague resource becomes a powerful and conscious reality that eventually becomes our core identity. But to move out of the shadow of the ego-self, we must have a conscious, direct experience of this spiritual dimension. As we shall see later, it is this experience, not intellectual insight, belief, or conviction that allows the identity to gradually shift from the ego-self to the spiritual-Self. As we advance in the journey of the warrior sage, the spiritual-Self becomes our only identity, an experienced sense of I-ness unlimited and undisturbed by the stresses and strains of everyday life. Of course, we still have an ego-self, but it is relegated to the role of manager of the mind/body complex, rather than the owner. The ego-self is employed as a servant to the higher spiritual-Self. Instead of the emotional habits and learned patterns of the ego, roles, or material things, we experience and define ourselves by the qualities of the spiritual-Self: love, compassion, humility, and joy.

The spiritual-Self is not simply a worthy ideal or some religious concept. We are not talking theory, but practical realities. How we experience our personal self determines our behavior and all aspects of our life. Family, work, social relationships, and leadership are all personal acts, determined by who we are, not by the beliefs we spout.

In other words, it's not what we *say*, it's what we *do* that counts. All too often, these are very different from each other. After all, fear, worry, and greed are far more powerful determinants of human behavior than professed "moral" or "religious" beliefs and values. If we experience ourselves as weak, we act out of fear and prejudice, lashing out at those whom we see as threatening. And these "threatening" people are always seen as "different," as non-believers, as un-American, or whatever the designated epitaph happens to be.

On the other hand, if we experience the inner strength, love, and freedom of the spiritual-Self, we become fearless, creative, and adaptive to change and difference. We are not driven to harm others in "pre-emptive" wars, impose our beliefs on others, or enslave them to unfair economic policies and pressures. To the degree that we become spirit-centered in our identity rather than ego-centered, we act in harmony with the finest qualities of the human spirit.

It is not a matter of either-or, but rather one of dominance. We are never without the spiritual core, nor can we function without an ego. What determines our thoughts, speech, and action is the degree to which either center – the ego or the spiritual core – dominates our sense of I-ness or identity. The more ego-centered we are, the more we are dominated by our habits, fears, and desires. The more spirit-centered we become, the more humane, compassionate, and balanced we are. As you might suspect, there are significant and powerful differences between being spirit-centered and being ego-centered, particularly as one or the other center becomes more dominant. We can briefly summarize some of the more significant differences between being spirit-centered and ego-centered in the following table. Be aware that the table is only meant to illustrate a few of the more extreme differences between the two, and is certainly not definitive of either condition.

Table 1:1

Spirit-Centred	Ego-Centred
Inner-directed: follows one's conscience	Seeks popularity, tries to anticipate what might be popular
Service orrientation; leader as servant	Ego-centred: leader as hero
Delegates, gives power away	Struggle for turf, power, fame, wealth (bigger, better, Number One)
Empowers others	Seeks ever-more power, influence
Acts with integrity	Takes every advantage
Concern with principles	Concern with winning
Humble; avoids spotlight	Arrogant; seeks credit, adulation
Fearless; genuinely self-confident	Driven by fears, tendency to violence

Even as we engage the warrior sage journey, we often move back and forth between identities. For most, the ego-self remains the dominant identity, but we still experience the subtle power of the spiritual-Self, and express these qualities in day-to-day activities. Not all ego-centered individuals are ego-maniacs, just as not all spirit-centered individuals are skilled and effective in their work or as leaders. There is, for example, a wide range of ego-centered leaders, from very skilled, caring and supportive leaders to raving ego-maniacs. There are ego-centered individuals who develop and express their spirit-centered qualities. These are, after all, human qualities, and a healthy ego will embrace these qualities. However, without the benefit of spiritual awareness, these qualities can fade, self-doubts and fears can overwhelm, and stress can lead to poor judgment and destructive behavior. For the ego-self, success all too easily leads to aggrandizement, and with great success – authority, power, or wealth – the ego becomes inflated and diseased. The famed English historian of liberty and freedom, Lord Acton, wrote "Power tends to corrupt and absolute power corrupts absolutely." This simple statement accurately defines an overwhelming reality for the ego-self.

Only the inner strength of the spiritual-Self can resist the powerful temptations of power and authority. In the light of spiritual awareness, the temptations of the material world hold no attraction. For the spirit-centered individual, these temptations simply do not exist. If you do not have a desire for power, wealth, name, and fame, they exist only as means to an end, not as ends in themselves. Without the inner strength of the spiritual-Self, the ego-self faces an almost certain risk of becoming destructive.

On the other hand, simply being rooted in the spiritual-Self does not guarantee that one develops the skills and abilities crucial to being successful in modern life nor for effective leadership. If you want to become a monk and retreat from the world in a hermit's hut on Mount Athos or in an ashram in India, then developing the powers and skills of the ego-self will be insignificant. But those of us who choose to live in the world, both the spiritual-Self and the ego-self are vitally necessary if we want to fulfill the promise of our humanity. This is why we speak of the dual aspect of personal greatness – the warrior and the sage. We must create a healthy ego and gain access as well as develop the inner skills of the mind/body complex if we want success in the world, and particularly if we want to become a skilled leader. But the ego-self must be constrained by service to the spiritual-Self; otherwise, we are in constant danger of suffering from the weaknesses of the human ego.

Lessons by Example

We have two outstanding examples from the last century that provide us with a clear lesson of the differences between being ego-centered or spirit-centered: Adolph Hitler and Mohandas Gandhi. These represent two extremes of personal development, and clearly illustrate radically divergent personal and leadership qualities as well as radically different outcomes. Hitler is an extreme example of the very worst of ego-centered leadership (historically, the list of these types of despots seems endless – Stalin, Mao, Pol Pot, Idi Amin, General Pinochet (Kim Il Sung of North Korea and Saddam Hussein are just a few of the more recent ones) – while Gandhi represents a wonderful example of spirit-centered leadership. (Unfortunately, we can add far more names of so-called leaders to Hitler's end of the continuum than Gandhi's.)

Both started political parties, provided leadership to their nations, and both influenced world events within the same time period. Both were charismatic, and both became powerful leaders who changed world realities. But the methods, accomplishments, and consequences of these two leaders were very different indeed, and they arise out of very different inner human qualities.

Hitler embraced violence and ruled through fear. He was obsessed with militarism, "heroic struggle," and war. These lay at the core of his disturbed ego, and became his controlling creed. His politics and religion were based on exclusion as he ranted and raved about the terrible "vermin Jews" and communists contaminating the pure Aryan race.

Hitler's power as an individual arose from his negative emotions: fear, self-hatred, and the hatred of others. He reached into the minds of the German people and galvanized their fears and hatreds. He created scapegoats for these frustrations and fears, while gaining political power through hatred, fear, and violence. His politics and his view of the world reflected his own twisted, distorted personality. Hitler lived by the power of the lie: "The great masses of the people … will more easily fall victims to a big lie than to a small one." (*Mein Kampf,* 1933). Driven by his fears and his lust for power, Hitler created destruction and human misery beyond belief. He exerted enormous influence by appealing to the very worst in people, and wanted the world to "obey" his master race.

In contrast, Gandhi embraced nonviolence. His was the politics of inclusion and compassion. Gandhi's political and personal power arose from the power of the human spirit rather than the needs of the human ego, and his message was about fearlessness and self-control. Gandhi transformed the world, bringing out the very best in both the Indian and the British people. In an expression of selflessness and service, the spirit drove him. Gandhi lived by, and influenced others through the principles reflecting the transformative power of the human spirit. Through these principles, Gandhi brought hope and self-determination for a great nation and a legacy that continues to influence today.

These principles were:

1. *Swaraj:* which means, "rule over oneself" or self-mastery. Gandhi firmly believed that the only true freedom arose from self-knowledge and self-discipline, the key aspects of self-mastery. In other words, Gandhi believed that people should, and could, rule themselves. For Gandhi, swaraj or self-mastery was the way to become free from illusion, ignorance, and fear. Ultimately, as Gandhi's life illustrates, self-mastery leads to spiritual-Self realization and the recognition of one's spiritual-Self in all others. Political freedom means nothing without this personal freedom. Swaraj was the foundation of everything Gandhi believed and lived.

2. *Satya:* which means the pursuit of truth. Gandhi did not claim to know the truth, only that he was in constant search for it, and in service to it. The highest truth for Gandhi was spiritual truth, and the inter-connectedness of all life. Gandhi understood this to be the meaning of the biblical phrase "The truth shall set you free," and that truth is a practical and obtainable reality for every human being. This realization was the foundation for his next principle, non-violence.

3. *Ahimsa:* which means non-violence. For Gandhi, non-violence was the means and truth was the ends, and these two could never be separated. Gandhi abhorred violence, and would never accept violence in thought, word, or deed to justify any goal or ends. For Gandhi, "As ye sow so shall ye reap" was his creed both personally and politically. His refusal to turn to violence characterized his entire political life, and brought the British Empire to its knees.

4. *Satyagraha:* this is a term coined by Gandhi referring to the power generated by truth and nonviolence. This is the force that substitutes for violence. In liberating love and compassion, the power of the human spirit, we have a power far stronger than hate and fear. It was this power that fueled Gandhi's leadership. Through his dedication to truth and nonviolence, Gandhi became fearless. He conquered the British not with military might, but with the irresistible power of his spiritual force. Gandhi never even had a police force, let alone an army.

5. *Sarvodaya:* which means equality. Gandhi insisted on equality between all classes. His spiritual experience taught him that the highest

truth was the essential unity of humanity. This spiritual truth is achieved through self-knowledge and self-discipline. In light of this truth, Gandhi believed that those with privilege must develop a sense of responsibility to use their wealth for the betterment of all, and the less privileged must lift themselves out of deprivation.

Through nonviolent actions, economic and social equality can be reconciled with individual freedom built on this spiritual truth. Genuine freedom demanded self-mastery – a personal freedom from fear, greed and violence. After achieving this mastery, political freedom, social equality, and economic security could be enjoyed by all levels of society.

It is important to understand that Gandhi *lived* the principles that he preached. His was a life of simplicity, integrity, and commitment to his principles and to all humanity. He was a living example of the qualities and principles he endorsed. How many leaders today do you know that live a simple, non-materialistic life, who are examples of the principles they supposedly embrace? Instead, our leaders – economic, political, and religious – talk about values but are driven by materialistic desires for profit, position, and power. How many leaders actually have the integrity to walk their talk rather than ride in limos of privilege?

No greater contrast can be found in both personal and leadership qualities than between Hitler and Gandhi. Both were human beings, both were effective, both used the powers of their mind. But Hitler was more like a rabid animal, a true egomaniac, ruthlessly giving vent to the most destructive of human emotions. He was a destructive, fearful human being, driven by fears and hatreds. Although he was militaristic, and fervently believed in military power and force, Hitler would never be considered as a warrior in any of the great traditions of martial arts. He was nothing more than an efficient killer, what the samurai of Japan contemptuously referred to as a mere sword fighter.

On the other hand, Gandhi was the genuine warrior – fearless, strategic, and decisive – but more than that, he was also a great sage – compassionate, visionary, and wise. Like the greatest of martial artists, Gandhi fervently believed in non-violence, and he placed his ego with all its emotional power in service of his spiritual-Self. Gandhi's greatest weapon in the struggle for independence and freedom was himself. His humanity – body, mind, and spirit – were his tools. Gandhi never complained about not having a level playing field, he skillfully adapted to any conditions that the British created and used them for his advantage. He skillfully used his ego and the powers of his mind in service to his spiritual-Self, and in that way, benefited the entire society.

Both men were powerful leaders, and both had great impact. But which qualities would you as an individual rather have? Which of these two would you encourage your children to follow? Which would you rather have as your friend and neighbor? Which one would you rather have as your leader?

The Uncommon Common Person

We use Hitler and Ghandi, powerful, famous leaders, to illustrate the enormous difference between a leader who is spirit-centered and one driven by the ego-self. But the reality is that most of us will never be in the position of national leader. A high-profile position of leadership is not the relevant point, however. The key is what serves as the foundation of our personal sense of identity: the powerful spiritual-Self or the weak and susceptible ego-self? What truly counts in everyday life isn't how powerful you are as a leader, but how powerful you are in your humanity.

Dick Roberts is certainly not someone who dominates the national news. He isn't even famous in the small town he calls home. Yet everyday, Dick lives a life of service, using his inner resources skillfully in his chosen profession as a math teacher in the local high school. His unique contribution is his refined spiritual sense, and his willingness to serve his students. Dick is revered by students, not only for his obvious concern for their well-being, but also for the joy, insight, and skilled intervention that he offers to each and every one that approaches him. Dick is unremittingly positive about his students, even when they are making choices that are harmful to themselves and possibly others. He holds them responsible for their actions without blaming them, and without diminishing their humanity for the mistakes they may make.

A skilled math teacher, Dick also brings a lifetime of self-mastery study and application to his students, providing them with the tools they need to access their own inner strengths. Life hasn't been easy for Dick and his family. He and his wife selflessly cared for their second son, Timmy, stricken by Tay-Sacs disease, until his death at age seven. Their third son suffers from a degenerative neural condition that will, in all likelihood, deprive him of the use of his legs by the age of thirty. Yet Dick faces each challenge with an inner peace and joy that allows him to reach out to his community and students with strength and service. He asks for nothing, and gives everything in return. For those who know him, he is a constant source of inspiration. If you listen to Dick for just a few minutes, you hear the power of the spiritual-Self flowing through the strong and healthy ego that engages the grateful community surrounding him.

His personal philosophy sustains and directs his every action. Born in a Jewish family, Dick has gone far beyond the dogmas and beliefs of any religion. Like Ghandi and Martin Luther King, Dick is guided by his spiritual experience, recognizing that there is only one human family, and that each individual is nothing less than another expression of the divine. His approach to life is both universal and particular. He has his own beliefs, but he respects the beliefs of others, knowing that in the final equation, we are all parts of one reality. No one would ever accuse Dick of not having an ego. Dick suffers from what he refers to as his obsessive rebellion dysfunction. In other words, he hates being told what to do by administrators and others in authority. But he maintains a tight rein on his ego-self, never compromising his spiritual realities of compassion, joy, and love in order to serve anger or resentment. Even in his frustration, Dick can laugh at himself and the situations his ego-self creates for him.

As unique an individual as Dick is, he certainly isn't alone. Look around and you will find inspiring individuals in every walk of life. These spirit-centered people are often quietly going about their life, working to create a better world for themselves and others. They travel to Central America to build homes or provide free dental surgery. They build schools in India, support children in the Philippines, and work to build conflict mediation services. They join the Peace Corps, join volunteer fire departments, and build homes with Habitat for Humanity.

They are deeply spiritual individuals who have no need to make others believe as they do. Instead of preaching to others about what to believe and how to live, they simply live as luminous models. Quiet, unassuming and effective, they are mostly ignored by a media that feeds on fears and frenzy. They may even be in positions of power, but this power is quietly and effectively expressed, away from the bright lights of the image-conscious media. They celebrate diversity, they encourage those who are struggling, and they lend a hand to those who have fallen, not because they can become famous for their philanthropy, but because they understand that we really are members of the one, same human family.

Look again at the qualities of the spirit-centered individual. These qualities aren't missing in our culture; they are simply not valued. Spirit-centered qualities don't make money, they don't bring fame, and they certainly don't amass power. But they are what make life worthwhile. We have a choice. We can continue on this path of suffering, tolerating, even supporting, ego-dominated leaders who grasp for power, wealth and fame, create "enemies" to justify military expansion, enrich the few at the top and economically enslave the many at the bottom with "trickle down" economics, and lead through fear and intimidation – or – we can develop ourselves as individuals who put their egos in service to, and derive their power from, the human spirit. We can be fully human, characterized by fearlessness and compassion, and inspire and lead others to freedom, self-knowledge, and self-discipline. We must, and can, become so strong that spirit-centered leadership emerges as the natural consequence of personal greatness. When the people live with strength, humility, compassion, and love, leaders will emerge that reflect these qualities of the people.

Gandhi was not a perfect human being. He made mistakes just as every human being does. However, Gandhi did strive to live his principles and to serve as a model for his beliefs. As a consequence, Gandhi lived his life with a joy that could not be destroyed by failure, by the death of his wife, or by the violence and conflict that was part of India's struggle. Fully human beings make mistakes, they laugh and cry, they succeed and fail. But through it all, they retain a quiet joy and contentment, an inner strength that arises from their spiritual-Self that sustains them through the most difficult of circumstances and times.

We certainly don't need to worship Gandhi, or any human being, but we should honor his humanity and respect the qualities that he personified by developing these same powerful, spirit-centered qualities within ourselves, in our families, and in our communities. Like Gandhi, Dick, and others, we can place the ego in service to our human spirit and become spirit-centered, skillful human beings. We can nurture and develop the warrior sage within ourselves, and access the powerful resources of the human spirit. But above all, we must demand these same qualities in those who aspire to be leaders.

We know the qualities of greatness; they lie embedded within the human spirit. Our quest is to realize these qualities within ourselves and develop them as conscious skills. This is not a matter of academic knowledge, theoretical models, going to school, or even changing our habits. It is, rather, both a transformational and a transcendent process, taking the resources we already have, and developing them as conscious skills and qualities. Transformation occurs as we access, develop, and refine the powerful innate capacities of the body/mind complex through self-mastery. Transcendence involves the shift of one's personal identity from ego-self to the transcendental spiritual-Self. Both transformation and transcendence are the result of inner awareness and growth, not of some vain attempt to change the personality. The point is that we don't have to become something different; we need to awaken the powerful mental and spiritual qualities we already possess deep within. We must become fully human. To accomplish this, we must turn to the human spirit itself, and access the power that lies within.

Chapter Two
The Spiritual Foundation

And yet, to me, what is this quintessence of dust?
—William Shakespeare's Hamlet—

What does it mean to be a human being? Our two historical examples in the last chapter, Adolph Hitler and Mohandas Gandhi, exemplify very different qualities. Obviously, we humans manifest a wide range of behaviors, characteristics, and qualities. We can be generous, helpful, and compassionate, and still at times be mean and petty. And we all touch upon personal greatness at one time or the other. Many of us have had a mystical experience of some kind, feeling that we are an essential part of something much greater than ourselves. But still, like Shakespeare's Hamlet, we wonder "… what is this quintessence of dust we call man?"

So what is the essential nature of the human being? There are as many beliefs as there are philosophies, scientific theories, and religious dogmas. Most of us, however, don't spend a great deal of time wondering about essential natures. Yet, how we relate to each other is determined very much by how we think of each other and ourselves. If we believe that human beings are essentially evil, nothing more than animals, we will focus on controlling this "animal nature." The classic political example of this is the infamous Machiavelli, the medieval

Italian political theorist. On the other hand, Plato, arguably the western world's greatest philosopher, believed that human nature was essentially pure and divine.

Like all of us, Machiavelli and Plato developed their political and philosophical beliefs and conclusions out of their personal experiences. Machiavelli, who lived in turbulent and violent times, advocated the use of raw power, claiming that any action is legitimate for a ruler, and that fear was a necessary tool for the prince. Hitler's leadership is a clear and unfortunate example of the very worst of Machiavelli's philosophy. Plato, on the other hand, who lived in the Golden Age of Greece, believed fervently that the essential criteria for any leader is a deep and profound love of knowledge, and that leaders should selflessly lead from the highest moral positions for the benefit of the people. Plato also argued for the equality of the sexes, a very radical position for his time. Obviously, Plato's experiences, as well as his philosophical and political beliefs, were quite different from Machiavelli's. Gandhi's view of human nature, as well as his leadership with its emphasis on personal responsibility, truthfulness, and equality, is an excellent example of Plato's philosophy and beliefs.

Following Plato and Gandhi, the view of the warrior sage is that human beings are the meeting point of the sacred with the profane, the infinite with the finite, and the spirit with the material. The essential nature of each human being is divine; it is a focused or circumscribed center of pure non-material Universal Consciousness, or God, that some call the soul, and that we refer to as the spiritual-Self. As a focused point of Universal Consciousness, the spiritual-Self is unlimited, unchanging, and eternal. The spiritual-Self is a reservoir of strength, joy, and love.

For the non-material spiritual-Self, the material reality of the personality, the mind/body structure with all its ego-self patterns and habits, is a tool to express itself and gain human experiences. The term "material" indicates that the mind/body complex that constitutes the personality is made of energy, and subject to change, death, and decay. The mind and its thoughts are subtle and illuminating energy; the life force is energizing and connects the mind and body; the energy of the body is dense and gross, the same as any physical object. From the point of view of the warrior sage, the mind/body complex, the entire personality, is a tool, a complex biocomputer, and mobile home for the spiritual-Self, the on-board representative of God.

When we use an automobile, it does not mean that we are the automobile. We will mistakenly say things like "I just had a flat tire," but what we really mean is that that the car had a flat tire. When we say we have a headache, what we really mean is that the head of the body hurts. And when we say we are angry, what we really mean is that the mind has angry thoughts. The ego-self takes over in all these instances, and creates a false and limited identity. When we live in these false and limited identities, we suffer the consequences. However, the spiritual-Self, the real "I" and the source of awareness and consciousness in the personality, doesn't suffer at all. We don't suffer or disappear when the automobile disintegrates; the spiritual-Self doesn't suffer or disappear when the body disintegrates.

What we call evil is not part of the core spiritual-Self, or consciousness, but rather a condition created through ignorance by the ego-self. Evil exists only as a temporary condition created by weaknesses inherent in the ego-self, and results in a loss of awareness (alienation) from the power, joy, and serenity of the spiritual-Self. These ignorant ego-self actions obscure the essential nature of the spiritual-Self and lead to suffering. But even the worst human evil cannot effect, damage, or alter the essential divinity of the spiritual-Self, which is the eternal heart of each individual.

This is illustrated by Figure 2:1. The infinity sign represents the dual aspect of the one human reality: the spiritual-Self and the material ego-self of the mind/body complex. The warrior sage, represented by the four-pointed star, is the successful integration of this dual nature of consciousness and matter so that the resources of both dimensions become conscious skills. For the warrior sage, the spiritual-Self empowers the mind/body complex of the ego-self, which, in turn, uses its resources to serve the spiritual-Self. Universal Consciousness is the unlimited, non-localized source, the indefinable God-head, represented by the sunburst as the origin of the spiritual-Self.

Figure 2:1

Warrior Sage

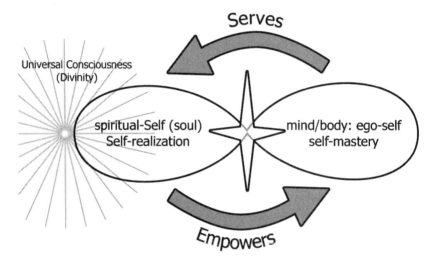

Each dimension brings unique capacities and abilities to task. The tools and methods necessary to access, refine, and enhance these resources, though different for each dimension, interpenetrate and reinforce each other. It is the singular achievement of the warrior sage to recognize, access, and integrate the powerful resources of both the spiritual core as well as the mind/body complex. This is a difficult and demanding task that involves a lifetime commitment to personal and continued learning.

Throughout history, this integration of body, mind, and spirit has been referred to as a quest, reflecting not only the greatness of the task, but also its danger and difficulty. We should recognize from the beginning that becoming a warrior sage is not easy. It is a practical and spiritual journey that takes all the strength we can muster. Even with the best of teachers and a supporting community, the journey is a solitary one. It is, literally, a struggle that each individual must make; each individual must face and conquer his own inner dragons, develop and refine his inner resources, and claim his rightful heritage. But every step we take makes us more effective in the world, and brings us greater peace, harmony, and joy.

What It Means to be Spiritual

When we hear the term "spiritual" or "spirituality," we aren't always clear as to what it means. Most people assume that we are talking about religious beliefs or some brand of philosophy. At that point, many people will quickly shy away, mumbling something about not talking about politics or religion. Discussions become heated as one person tries to convert the other to a particular religious belief.

But spirituality and spiritual skills are not the same as religion or religious beliefs. Spirituality and religion are often related to each other, and as we achieve spiritual knowledge we enhance and deepen religious beliefs. But they are different realities, and it is not a necessary connection. Religion needs spirituality if it is to be genuine, but spirituality does not need religion, nor does it need to be expressed in a religious belief.

Our approach here is simple and direct. Spirituality is the conscious experience (awareness) and expression of the core qualities that characterize the human spirit, the very best of human expression. It is not what we believe, or what we claim, that makes us spiritual, but rather what we experience and what we do. The spiritual experience is transcendental in its very nature. To transcend means to experience a sense of self beyond the normal experience of the mind/body complex of the ego-self. This transcendent experience is also transformative. In other words, a spiritual experience changes not only how we see ourselves, but who we are and how we think and behave.

The terms "spiritual" and "spirituality" are used in many ways, but if we look at the great sages of all traditions, we find universal qualities that transcend culture, time, and beliefs. Regardless of the particular religious tradition or culture, the great sages of all traditions share universal qualities that define spirituality.

These are:

• A realization that divinity is one and the same in all. This results from the direct, conscious experience that the underlying reality within each and every living expression is the same one reality. It is the recognition that we are all expressions of the same universal God. As long as this statement remains nothing more than a belief, spirituality is incomplete. As we shall see later, it is the direct experience of this truth that is the *sine quo non* of spirituality. All other qualities of spirituality arise from this realization.

• A search for truth rather than a claim to have it. The term "truth" here refers to the direct experience of divinity, not a set of beliefs or dogmas. The full truth can't be found in the beliefs of any science, philosophy, or religion. These so-called "truths" are perspectives, ways of describing aspects of the universal God-head. No belief system contains the complete truth in and of itself. It is delusional arrogance to think that any religion, philosophy, or science alone knows the singular immensity of the God-head, or that any belief system can encapsulate it. Those who claim to have the singular truth delude themselves, mistaking beliefs for truth. Almost always, these individuals have closed minds, filled with fear, and dislike anything that differs from their belief system. More importantly, they fail to acquire the other universal qualities that define spirituality.

• A respect for the life force. To be spiritual is to respect the life force – in others, in the environment, in the food we eat – in all expressions of the life force. The realization that God, or divinity, is the underlying reality (the truth) of all existence brings a deep appreciation for the diversity of life. When we judge and condemn others and their beliefs, we create a separation between ourselves and that core identity, which more often than not, leads to an evil will to eliminate those who don't agree with us.

• An understanding that every action has its consequences. This is expressed as the Biblical phrases "As ye sow so shall ye reap," or "Those who live by the sword die by the sword," and the Vedic concept of the law of karma. In other words, there is a deep awareness and appreciation that love brings love and violence brings violence. Because of this, truly spiritual individuals take care not to harbor hatreds, greed, or violence in their hearts and minds, recognizing that it simply leads to further hatreds, greed, and violence.

• An appreciation of all paths to the Divine. Spiritual beings recognize that any religious path can be valid, and that there are many ways to express spiritual experience. They recognize that beliefs are nothing more than beliefs, tools of the mind, and not truth. This leads to openness and a celebration of diversity, rather than the closed-mindedness and fanaticism of fundamentalism.

• A dedication to eliminate suffering and serve others. Spiritual individuals are compassionate, and work to alleviate the suffering of others. They know that love is the singular expression of the divine, and strive to express that divinity in all that they do. They live simple lives, uncomplicated by greed, possessiveness, and the need for fame, fortune, and power. They own nothing in their minds, thus they are owned by nothing. They are free spirits, moving in the world without attachments, shame, or glory.

These qualities vary in expression from individual to individual, but characterize all great spiritual individuals. The foundation is the direct realization (experience) of a transcendent personal identity, free from the dictates of needs, fears, and other habits that constitute the ego-self. As we shall see, this spiritual identity is necessarily and exclusively grounded in direct experience and not dependent on the beliefs and patterns that characterize the ego-self.

The ego-self is necessarily structured by genetics, culture, beliefs, and language – all the things that go into constructing the uniqueness of each individual. On the other hand, the spiritual-Self lies at the core of what it means to be human, regardless of culture, race, creed, or even time. While the unique characteristics of the ego-self certainly determine how we express our spiritual experiences, the spiritual experience itself is universal to all human beings, and thus the common core of all human experience. When we say that this experience is universal, it does not mean that every individual has this experience, only that the spiritual core is within every individual, and each individual has the potential of consciously experiencing this spiritual core. Whether or not we have the conscious experience depends on many factors such as neural development, self-knowledge, self-discipline, and access to a transcendental tradition or discipline.

The critical fact of spirituality, as well as its verification, lies in direct, conscious experience of this universal spiritual-Self, not in any belief, creed, or cultural frame. Without direct experience of this core reality, there is no substance to the word "spiritual." There are various terms for this experience – samadhi, satori, buddhahood, Christ-consciousness, enlightenment – depending on culture and tradition. In western culture, this experience is often referred to as a "mystical" experience.

The Mystical Experience: Practical Spirituality

Spirituality begins with, and is sustained by, an inner and immediate *experience* of a transcendent Self. The conscious awareness of this transcendent Self is often referred to as a "mystical experience" because it defies logical explanation or definition. It remains a "mystery" to the human mind. Mystical experiences and near-death experiences, though not identical, share the same experience of a transcendent spiritual-Self through very different means.

While the experience lies beyond the capacity of the mind to define or explain it, it is certainly within our capacity to have it. The experience itself removes any and all doubt about the reality of the spiritual essence as it opens the heart and leads to an overwhelming sense of love, compassion, and fearlessness. Those who don't have this experience, particularly some who call themselves scientists, create all sorts of theories to explain away the mystical experience of others. They use terms such as "illusions," "brain states," and "oxygen deprivation," claiming there is nothing "mystical" about them. It is interesting to note, however, that whenever one of these "scientists" has a genuine mystical experience, they immediately change their beliefs and no longer advocate their original limited concepts.

The impact of this direct experience of the spiritual-Self far transcends any intellectual, religious, or philosophical belief. The power lies in the experience and nowhere else.

Belief versus Experience

It is this freedom from the limits of the conditioned mind that resides at the heart of the spiritual experience. Spirituality is not, and cannot be, defined by a belief or dogma. We may talk about our spiritual experiences, we may celebrate them in formal ways, and we may certainly communicate about them within a particular cultural framework, using words that communicate concepts and ideas to others. But words only describe the experience; they are not the experience itself. They are symbols, mere representations of the experience.

We may talk about being hungry, we may even think about being hungry, but hunger itself is not a thought or concept; it is an experience. What moves us to satisfy our hunger is the experience of hunger, not the thought of being hungry. Similarly, what moves us to love others is the experience of loving that arises from the spiritual-Self, not the concept, belief, commandment, or injunction that we must love each other. Many religious people believe that they should love their enemies, but how many are actually capable of following that religious injunction? Most people have difficulty loving anyone that is different from them, let alone someone they think might be an enemy. The fact is that religions have been, and continue to be, the source of much conflict, war, terrorism, domination and suffering.

Words, beliefs, and dogmas necessarily limit experience. The power of spirituality lies not in a certain set of beliefs, but in a deepening of wisdom and knowledge acquired through direct experience. We must be careful not to let beliefs and concepts limit our spiritual experience. If we have only the words, if we operate only on belief, we limit our experience and cannot access the transformative and transcendent power of the spiritual-Self. To the extent that we allow beliefs to limit experiences, we limit our capacity to grow, solve problems, be creative, and understand the world around us. In short, we limit our success at being human; we certainly limit our success with greatness.

The power of experience over concepts and beliefs is easy to understand. Let's say, for instance, that you must undergo very delicate brain surgery, and you have the choice of two doctors. Dr. Smith has just graduated first in his class from Harvard Medical School and had the highest score on the medical exams. He has just completed a surgical internship and has participated in a few operations similar to yours, knowing all about them from his studies.

On the other hand, Dr. Brown went through medical school over thirty years ago, had average grades, and medicine has changed drastically since he was in school. Dr. Brown has successfully performed over 2,000 surgeries, without a single failure, just like the one you need. Which would you choose?

Most of us would choose Dr. Brown's experience over Dr. Smith's intellectual knowledge. Of course, it might be worthwhile to have Dr. Smith assist Dr. Brown, and have the benefit of both. This is similar to the role the mind (and it's religious, philosophical, or scientific beliefs) plays in relation to the spiritual experience. The power is in the experience, and the mind (with its various beliefs and concepts) helps us to organize, celebrate, and share that experience.

If mere beliefs dominate, such as we find in religious, philosophical, and scientific dogmas and institutions, then spiritual experience is inhibited and may even be dismissed as fantasy. When religion is divorced from the experience of the spiritual-Self, it becomes ego-centered. Ego-centered religions are nothing more than political organizations primarily interested in using "God" to control others by claiming exclusivity (We are the one true religion), promote divisiveness (We are saved; the rest will go to hell), and trade on fears (You better do what the religious leader says), all of which lead to hostilities, and even war. The same can be said about any belief system – political, scientific, philosophical, etcetera. The moment we confuse beliefs with truth, we limit our possibilities, our greatness, and ourselves.

A genuine mystical or spiritual experience transcends the human mind and its limits dictated by learning, culture, race, gender, and nationality. The experience of this spiritual-Self varies according to the depth and competency of the individual having the experience, but ultimately, it is the same in all people, in all philosophies, in all religions. Of course it is expressed differently because the minds that interpret the experience differ according to culture, beliefs, and language.

The spiritual essence, or Self, is often, but not necessarily, experienced as light. That is why many spiritual traditions use light to represent the divine. Whether we call that essence the soul, the spiritual-Self, or simply the human spirit, is totally irrelevant. *What is critically relevant is that we experience this powerful, practical dimension of our humanity, and recognize this same reality in others.* While fundamental to all religions, spirituality and truth are not restricted to, or the sole purview of, any particular belief system.

Religion: Coloring the Light

Religions begin in the teachings of great sages who try to communicate the power, beauty, and truth of their own spiritual wisdom and knowledge to those who do not yet have their own experience of spiritual wisdom and knowledge. Often the greatest of these sages become the focal point of religious beliefs, such as Jesus, Buddha, or Mohammed.

Religion is the formalization or codification of spiritual experience, knowledge, and wisdom. Religious beliefs and practices may be intended to inspire, guide, or direct the individual to a spiritual realization, but the belief itself is not the experience. As we have said, it is only a representation. We can understand religion, then, as a formalized attempt to interpret and communicate spiritual experiences within a common cultural framework.

Genuinely spiritual individuals are universal. That is, they respect the religious beliefs of all peoples. They do not impose their religious beliefs on others since they realize that the same spiritual core exists within in all people. They know that religious beliefs, which belong to the ego-self, only color the pure light of the spiritual-Self. Before being colored by the filter of religious beliefs, the pure light of spirituality is the same in everyone. Spirituality may or may not wear a religious cloak. Many spiritual individuals do not endorse a particular religious belief, while others are very engaged in a particular religion. The great sages and true saints of all religions were, and are, deeply spiritual beings. Their lives and personalities reflect the joy and wisdom of conscious spirituality.

Religions, however, are created within the uniqueness of human minds, which are conditioned by the limitations of culture, experience, and time. What seems true and meaningful to one time and culture will seem trivial and untrue in another time to a different culture. When religious beliefs and dogma become more important than the spiritual experience, we lose touch with our common spiritual core. Differences are magnified and conflict ensues. Then religious beliefs become self-imposed limitations and we are back in the world of diversity problems, fear, prejudice, and bigotry. All of which inhibit knowledge, performance, and effectiveness.

Only the *experience* of union transcends polarities, concepts and beliefs. The experience *is* the transformational process that brings out personal greatness, not belief, intellectual effort, or scientific theory. Direct awareness of the spiritual-Self, the mystical experience, *is* the transcendent event out of which greatness emerges.

By grounding religious beliefs in spiritual experience, we become free of petty prejudices that interfere with the ability to communicate with others different from ourselves. This gives us the freedom to learn from others, to work effectively with other cultures and beliefs, and create opportunities for mutual growth and benefit. Then religious expression finds innumerable ways to express itself, adding to the richness and creativity of every individual.

There is no doubt that the real power of our humanity lies within the human spirit. There are many ways to talk about it. Physicist David Bohm speaks about the implicate order. Joseph Chilton Pearce speaks about the evolution and the development of neo-cortical potential. The great Persian poet Kabir says that the drop becomes the ocean and the ocean realizes itself as that drop. The Bible speaks endlessly about love, and India's *Rig Veda* says that "in the beginning was love…" The analogies are endless, but the experience is universal.

The Warrior Sage: A Spirit-Centered Life

Even the most rigid belief system can be changed by the power of the human spirit. And when our lives are guided by the human spirit, rather than the ego, we become individuals who truly serve others, foster self-control rather than domination, and live with compassion rather than prejudices and hatreds. The qualities of a spirit-centered life are not only powerful (recall that Gandhi never even had a police force, let alone relied on military power), but inspire a spiritual transformation in those who come into contact with it. Martin Luther King exerted enormous influence, not through the power of weapons, but through the power of love, through the power of the human spirit. Many may argue that Ghandi and King ultimately failed to accomplish their goals. They point out that there is still racial violence and disharmony in the United States, and point to the political corruption, social prejudices, and the violence found in India today. But did they fail, or does the failure lie in those that followed, and in the people themselves? Spirit-centered individuals provide the model and inspire by example, but they cannot force anyone to transform.

There is no doubt that the more spirit-centered we become the more humane, the more compassionate, and the more effective we become. Both King and Gandhi are examples of the warrior sage, an individual characterized by a deep respect for life. The term "warrior sage" was chosen with great care because it delineates leadership characterized by applied spirituality. The warrior leader who is not also a sage often ends up being a disaster for his or her followers. The human ego, even with the best of intentions, is easily corrupted by power, fame, and fortune.

Contrary to the warrior leader, the warrior sage is spirit-centered. The ego-self remains an integral part of the mind, but it is employed in service to the spiritual-Self. The true warrior sage is adverse to war and violence. He is a person of thoughtful, skillful action in a world filled with danger of all kinds. He represents personal integrity and honor built on self-discipline and control, fearlessness, strategic capacity and clarity of thought, decisiveness, and will. Adaptable, flexible, and focused, the warrior sage represents the practical application of inner skills.

Life demands strength. The weak are brutalized by both their own inner dragons of fear and self-hatred as well as by external dragons: the fears, greed, and violence of others. We need a warrior mentality not only for the terrorists, criminals, powerful individuals who seek to take advantage for their own benefits, the hysteria of the crowd, and the ennui of modern life, but also for the more subtle, more powerful inner enemies – the greed, the lust for power, and the fear (instigated by the terrorist, manipulated by the politician, and trumpeted by the media). The greatest danger to freedom, which is absolutely essential for spiritual unfoldment, is not external enemies, but the ignorance, the apathy, and the fear that lies within us. The warrior sage is far more concerned with these inner dragons than he is with the outer dragons.

The powerful mind (intellect) of the warrior is incomplete without an equally powerful spirit (heart/intelligence). The sage represents the powers and qualities that arise from the human spirit, or spiritual-Self. Along with the fearlessness, will, and instincts of the warrior, we need the wisdom, clarity, and compassion of the sage. These are the qualities that signify greatness, and these are the very qualities most lacking in western culture. We have plenty of warriors, but they act most often for their own egos. Their true motivation is to win, to gain as much as they can. In their mind, others exist only to feed their frenzied needs for power.

Whereas the warrior achieves self-mastery, the sage achieves Self realization, a conscious on-going awareness of the spiritual-Self. The sage is characterized by compassion, wisdom, and a deep respect for life in all its aspects. She experiences the inner-connectedness of life, and lives in, and with, harmony both within and without. Winning and losing are understood as simply part of the dance of life, and the goal is self-expression, freedom, and knowledge. The sage remains indifferent to evil, and thus retains balance and clarity of mind. In this way, she remains effective regardless of circumstance, and is a living model for those who follow.

Gandhi was a successful leader because he was a spiritual human being. He wasn't born a sage or leader, nor was he an imposing figure. But Gandhi lived his principles, and he masterfully used his personality (ego-self) as an instrument to accomplish his goals. His personal power, expressed through a strategic mind, an indomitable will, and skillful actions, arose from his central principal of *swaraj*, or self-mastery, the skill and knowledge to rule over one's own thoughts, speech, and actions. Through self-mastery, Gandhi developed the skills of an accomplished warrior. These alone would make him, or anyone, a force to be reckoned with.

But the personal power that characterizes Gandhi as a warrior emerges from a far deeper source than the ego-self. The warrior's personal power is only the reflection of the unlimited, universal power of the spiritual-Self. Gandhi held an uncompromising commitment to truth and non-violence, along with a compassionate dedication to equality and the welfare of all. He showed the same respect for British life that he had for Indian life. His compassion was universal, his principles were universal, and his actions were universal. Gandhi wanted the best for all peoples, including the British. For Gandhi, all were God's children, not just the people of his country, his race, or his belief.

Gandhi had a strong, healthy ego, and it was in service to his spiritual-Self. Gandhi clearly led his people, and he took full responsibility for making decisions. But his decisions were always in point of service – to provide opportunity, not to exert control. He was fully committed to his spiritual principles, and was willing to give his life for them. In so doing, he successfully integrated the individual power of the material self and the universal power of the spiritual-Self, becoming an irresistible force that could not be denied.

We can make the same choices. *The Warrior Sage* provides a framework of inner methodologies that can be used for the development, integration, and union of the body, mind, and spirit. To transform anything is to bring out a powerful, new expression from what is already there. When we live with the intent of transforming ourselves, we engage spiritual power and develop innate strengths and capabilities through self-knowledge and self-discipline. This is an inner-directed, inner-focused evolutionary process of growth in which unlimited strength arises from the human spirit, finds creative formulation through the human mind, and skillful expression through effective action. Transformation is a natural, organic process that occurs as a natural consequence of using the right tools. This spiritual way of life leads to fearlessness, compassion, and harmony. It fosters the spiritual qualities of the individual, the community, the organization, and the nation. Becoming a warrior sage is not a question of belief or concept, but a matter of direct experience created through self-training and practice. The potential for growth is unlimited, unique to each individual, and determined solely by one's commitment and willingness to practice. The only limitations are the ones we create and impose on ourselves.

This is the practical application of Gandhi's concept of swaraj, rule over one's own, or self-mastery through Self realization. It is not a matter of style, or learning how to influence others, but a way of life leading to personal, professional, and social fulfillment. It requires a committed, systematic approach with the tools and conceptual frameworks that lead to self-knowledge and skill. That means that we must learn to take control of our inner resources, including the ego, and use our personality as a conscious tool.

Traditional education provides little, if any, preparation for this task. And this is one of the great weaknesses of modern education. We tell our children what to do but don't show them how. We tell our children to control their emotions, but don't give them the tools necessary to do so. We teach our children what to think, but not how to use the mind. But the greatest tragedy in modern education is that we don't give our children (or ourselves) the tools we need to access their inner strength, the power of the human spirit. We don't provide our children with the inner technology necessary to develop the spiritual, mental, and physical power inherent in their own humanity.

What makes this even more difficult is that there is very little support for this quest in modern culture. The materialism and conformity of modern culture are powerful obstacles. Even worse is a "fast food" mentality that demands that any achievement be fast and easy. The self-help pop-psychology industry promises all sorts of skills, abilities, and even enlightenment with little effort and often within thirty days. After all, spiritual mastery only needs a good seminar and the right mantra, or better yet, a touch on the head with a peacock feather. Add to this religious fundamentalism and you have the recipe for the difficulties that characterize modern culture.

Western culture does not encourage inner growth, and formal

education does not prepare us for this journey. This means that we must find the way for ourselves. Fortunately, the knowledge, tools, and techniques necessary for this journey are available through a number of different traditions and disciplines that recognize the spiritual foundation of human nature. We can engage this quest and successfully complete it. But like any journey, it helps if we have clarity about where and how the journey takes place.

The quest for the warrior sage follows the dual nature of the human experience. We must build a foundation in Self realization, becoming aware of the spiritual-Self, and at the same time, become skilled in self-mastery, disciplining and refining the ego-self, and acquiring skill with the powerful resources of the mind/body complex. Through self-awareness and self-training, we access and enhance the powerful inner resources of the mind/body structure. This is the "way" or "path" of the warrior sage.

This journey is both challenging and rewarding. To prepare ourselves for this challenge, we must gain some insight into the nature of spiritual awareness, or the mystical experience. In the next chapter we will explore the principles and the processes that are part of every spiritual pathway. This will give us the information we need to choose our way or path with clarity and confidence.

Chapter Three
Process–The Triangle of Power

You are the architect of your life and you decide your destiny.
—*His Holiness Swami Rama*—

The warrior sage represents the pinnacle of personal greatness: the culmination of self-mastery and Self realization. These are not separate events, but reinforcing, integral aspects of our humanity. We achieve Self realization only through self-mastery, and self-mastery is not complete until we achieve Self realization. The foundation of each individual, as well as our common humanity, is the universal spiritual core; but the gateway to that universal truth is through the uniqueness of the individual personality.

This is not to say that there is only one way to get to the pinnacle. Each individual must discover his or her own path which necessarily reflects the uniqueness of the individual ego-self. Human beings are open systems, capable of arriving at the same end through a variety of ways. To insist that there is only one way – only one tradition that is right, only one religion that is right, only one martial art that is right – is not just egotistical, but ego-maniacal. The ways to God are not limited; only ego-selves create limits.

Beliefs, concepts, and practices vary from culture to culture, time to time, and tradition to tradition. But underlying these differences are universal processes and principles that are the foundation of every spiritual and self-mastery tradition. For example, yoga breathing exercises are somewhat different than Tai Chi breathing exercises. However, both lead to increased control over energy and thought. The exercises or techniques are particular to each tradition, but the use of breathing for inner balance, increased energy and power, and greater control of emotion and thought, is universal. Christian beliefs and practices are different from Taoist beliefs and practices, but both are designed to facilitate spiritual experience and knowledge. They have different ways of worshipping, understanding, and experiencing the divine. But the same underlying elements – prayer, meditation, and contemplation – are utilized in both traditions.

Regardless of the tradition involved, personal greatness, with its source deep within the spiritual core, arises out of these universal human processes. Consequently, this is where we begin. Again, it doesn't matter how we refer to this spiritual core – soul, spirit, atman, a spark of God – it only matters that we engage in a systematic process to experience this source and access its power and knowledge as conscious skills. The more clearly we understand these principles and processes, the more clearly we grow within our chosen tradition and comfortably accept the validity of individual and cultural differences.

Universal Principles: Consciousness and the Triangle of Power

We begin our exploration with what might appear to be a statement of belief: the power that underlies human nature is infinite and eternal. This power is without beginning and without end, thus immeasurable. This one reality is called by various names in different cultures – God, Brahman, the Tao – but these names only designate this reality. This reality is also described in many different ways – the Father, Son, and Holy Ghost of Christianity, the *Satchitananda* (Existence, Consciousness, and Bliss) of Vedanta philosophy, the Unspeakable Name of Judiasm, or the supra-implicate order of physicist David Bohm. All are simply ways of ascribing aspects to a reality that remains beyond all name, description, and form. This supreme reality is the final cause of all material existence and change, and yet, itself, remains changeless.

It is the one reality from which all realities evolve, the one truth from which all truths evolve. It is pure intelligence, indestructible, and ever-present.

For our purposes here, we focus on this reality in its aspect of Universal Consciousness. We will use capital C when meaning Universal Consciousness. This Consciousness is *not* conscious mind, or the consciousness of "consciousness raising" groups. These are ego-self limited expressions of Consciousness. Universal Consciousness is all-pervasive, and cannot be categorized, broken into parts, analyzed, or detected by the most sophisticated technology. It is non-material, without form or structure. It is a-logical, and cannot be encapsulated by the logic of the mind. That being said, however, this Consciousness can be experienced, and that experience is the mystical experience described in Chapter 2. Universal Consciousness is not the mind, nor the limited consciousness of the mind. It is not the brain, nor does it arise from the brain. Universal Consciousness is the ultimate resource, the hidden, subtle universal Self inside every creature.

For most, the above statements remain only a belief. As such, it is simply one of many beliefs. Westerners, such as the materialist philosopher Dennet, author of *Consciousness Explained*, argue that ultimately, any statement about consciousness is a matter of faith or belief. This statement, however, belies his dependence on analytic reasoning. His arguments are based on logic and not direct experience, and simply are not relevant to Self realization, or mystical knowledge: the experience of Consciousness achieved through direct apprehension or awareness. The materialist's ignorance of mystical knowledge does not nullify or negate this knowledge. It only reflects the limited experience of the materialist.

By and large, Western science sees consciousness as an artifact of neural activity. John Searle, a highly respected philosopher at the University of California in a course called "The Philosophy of Mind," states that consciousness emerges from brain activity in the waking state. He states as a simple proof the "fact" that we are not conscious when we are in coma, dreaming, or in deep sleep. His assertion, as well as his "facts," are inaccurate, and reflect his lack of experience. Not only are many people conscious of conversations while they are in coma, many of us are fully conscious of our dreams, and, in fact, use that awareness as a way to alter and change dreams at will. When accomplished yoga practitioners perform yoga *nidra*, they remain fully conscious while in deep sleep, with their brain producing delta waves. This was demonstrated in a laboratory setting by the yoga master Swami Rama in a research project directed by Dr. Elmer Green at the Voluntary Controls Laboratory at the Menninger Clinic back in the early 1970's. There are documented accounts where individuals are clinically dead, yet remain fully conscious of what is happening around them, and report these activities in accurate detail.

As stated above, Consciousness cannot be analyzed or understood by the mind, but we experience it through spiritual-Self realization. Of course, there are various degrees of intensity and clarity, depending on one's skill with the universal principles and processes that bring about spiritual-Self realization. In the tantric tradition, these universal principles are symbolized by a sacred triangle that represents the principles of knowledge (*jnana*), will (*icca*) and action (*kriya*). The principles are universal and represent processes critically relevant to all levels of human experience. In the tantric tradition, these principles define the creative intelligence and power of the supreme, which is called *Shakti*.

On the personal level, these three principles lead to the experience and knowledge of both the spiritual-Self and the ego-self. As discussed in later chapters, these principles underlie the three spiritual paths of prayer (action), meditation (will) and contemplation (knowledge). On a practical level, these principles serve as the foundation for ego-self-mastery, material knowledge, and personal effectiveness. For the warrior sage, self-knowledge provides access to the subtle resources of the mind and body, the inner strength of a strong will provides the desire and determination necessary for accomplishment, and actions that are balanced and purposeful lead to success without creating stress and unnecessary conflict.

For our purposes, we will modify the triangle in order to include the evolution of the individual spirit from the Universal Spirit. The following illustration, Figure 3:1, represents these universal processes and principles.

In the diagram, Universal Consciousness (God, nature, divinity) is symbolized by the empty space in the center of the four-pointed star. This is the indefinable reality from which all things evolve. The four-pointed star represents the individual soul or spirit. This is the spiritual-Self, a limited center of consciousness (as opposed to unlimited Universal Consciousness) that constitutes the core of every human being. This is most often referred to as the soul. The spiral line emanating from the center of the space represents the power (*shakti*) of the all-pervasive God or Universal Consciousness to manifest a limited center of itself in a creative act of will. Out of this power (shakti) arises the material form of the mind/body complex.* The solid line forming the circle represents the physical mind/body complex, including the ego-self. This circle is simply an attempt to illustrate the underlying reality as it willfully manifests in a particular material form (i.e., a human, a dog, a tree). In other words, the Supreme Reality, or God, is the underlying source of all creation, not just the soul.

Figure 3:1

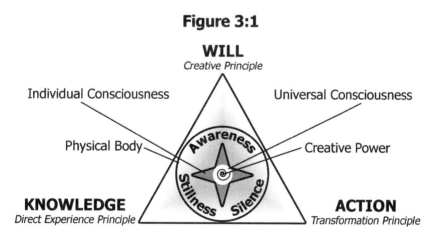

---

* The evolution of individual soul, mind, life-force, and body (matte) is defined in the very sophisticated philosophies of the tantric traditions, such as the Pratyabhijna Philosophy of Kashmir Saivism and the closely related philosophy of Saktadviatavada. For those interested, read *Fundamentals of the Philosophy of Tantras* by Manoranjan Basu and *Shakti and Shakta* by Arthur Avalon.

The terms "awareness," "stillness," and "silence" are the core processes by which the spiritual-Self and ultimately, the Universal Self, is experienced, or realized. Unless we expand our limited individual awareness through stillness and silence, we are unable to experience, i.e., be aware of, the greater Universal Consciousness. All spiritual paths, all inner technologies, if they are valid spiritual disciplines, lead to greater awareness through stillness and silence; otherwise, spiritual-Self realization cannot occur. The term "awareness" is, of course, directly related to the word "consciousness." To be aware of something is to be conscious of that thing. Awareness is the subjective experience of consciousness. Awareness is directed by attention to an object, whether that object is a material form, a mental form, or the spiritual form of the individual soul.

Universal Consciousness does not have a subjective experience because there is no subject/object duality. When a raindrop meets the ocean, the individual drop no longer exists as an individual drop, but now experiences itself as the ocean. The drop has become universal. Just so, as the individual consciousness (sense of I-ness) is merged into Universal Consciousness, the individual, subjective experience no longer exists as there is no subject/object duality. The experience is indescribable because it is beyond mind, but that does not negate its reality. Spiritual growth is an expansion of individual awareness from the limited "I" of the ego-self to the unlimited "I" of the spiritual-Self to the experience of Universal Consciousness, beyond subject/object duality.

The most useful practice is stillness. Stillness means that the neural fields are quieted, and all thought (whether we experience that thought as words, images, or sensations) is completely quieted. This sounds strange to western minds that are constantly active and seeking stimulation. But only through stillness can awareness be sufficiently refined to access the creativity, deep wisdom, and unlimited inner strength of the mind. Only through stillness do we become aware of the subtle resources of the mind and the spiritual core of our humanity. Stillness leads to silence. When all mental activity is quieted, when absolute calm pervades the mind-field, our limited awareness penetrates the barrier of the bioelectric field of the mind, expands to the subtle spiritual-Self, and Self realization is achieved. Again, this experience is not a logical process or event. It is not what we "think" that leads to Self realization, but what we experience. We must transcend the limits of mind and ego-self consciousness to gain this spiritual experience.

These three – awareness, stillness and silence, – are essential aspects of every spiritual tradition because they are necessary core processes of spiritual knowledge. All formal paths and inner technologies utilize methods and techniques that enhance these processes. The techniques and explanatory concepts vary from tradition to tradition, from culture to culture, but regardless of the approach or philosophy, they must engage these critical core processes.

The points of the encompassing triangle – the principles of knowledge, will and action – represent the evolutionary powers that not only define the evolution from Consciousness to individual being, but also reveal the ego-self and its inner resources as well as bring about the mystical experience, the revelation of the spiritual-Self and its universal source. Like the core processes, these principles, and the processes they represent, are essential to both self-mastery and Self realization. All three are necessary, and they are irrevocably intertwined. Having one without the other is like trying to eat milk with a fork. For example, knowledge without determination and skill leads to frustration and neurotic impotency. Full of theories and ideas, we still feel powerless, because we are. We are paper tigers who know what to do, but have no power to do it. These are the empty dreams, the broken promises, the unfulfilled resolutions – "I should have…would have…could have…" – that make up so much of everyday life.

A strong will without self-awareness breeds fanaticism and egomania. These are the politicians who lust for power and control and corporate executives who demand millions in compensation as they bankrupt the company. Actions taken without self-knowledge are dissatisfying as we end up with consequences that are not what we wanted. And without determination, nothing is ever finished, particularly when the going is tough. Each point of the power triangle reinforces the other two processes, and, in turn, is reinforced by the others. Keeping this in mind, let us briefly explore each principle of the power triangle.

Knowledge as Direct Experience

The principle of knowledge represents the power of direct experience. This is not intellectual knowledge, but knowledge gained as an internal process of change. It is "knowing from the inside out." Most of what we call knowledge is simply suggestion, something that someone has told us, that we have heard from a teacher, or read in a book. This is not direct knowledge, but suggestion. It has no power until we internalize it and experience it for ourselves.

We can speak of two levels – Self-knowledge (capital S), which is the mystical experience, or direct experience of the spiritual-Self and, eventually, the Universal Self; and self-knowledge (lower case s), which is inner knowledge of the ego-self and its resources. In Chapter 2, we saw that direct conscious awareness of the spiritual-Self, Self realization, is necessary to achieve the mystical experience.

The principle of direct experience also applies directly to the ego-self and its powerful resources. This is self-knowledge, the direct conscious apprehension and awareness of internal mental and physical events. This includes not only mental events, such as our thoughts and emotions, but also the ability to access on-going moment-to-moment physiological processes. Typically, we are only aware of a very small percentage of these on-going mental and physical events. Most operate well beyond normal levels of awareness. There is a practical reason for this. If we had to be fully conscious of every mental and physical event or process, we couldn't function efficiently, if at all. But this efficiency is also a trap. All too often we remain a slave to whatever habits we happen to develop as we grow. When this is the case, we only develop to the level that our habits allow. In other words, we rarely develop more than a very small percentage of our full capacities as human beings.

Medical experts estimate that as high as fifty percent of the American public suffers from high blood pressure. They also tell us that most individuals won't be aware of this because the symptoms are few and subtle. There may be only a few symptoms, and they may be subtle, but they are easily recognized if one knows how to be aware of them. Unfortunately, the lack of awareness often leads to serious consequences, even death. The truth is that the body is fully equipped with feedback mechanisms that reflect every physiological change, including blood pressure. These provide us the opportunity to recognize when our blood pressure goes too high, which, in turn, allows us to intervene and bring our blood pressure back to a healthy level. Our awareness of, and skill with, the control systems of the body easily allows us to stabilize blood pressure through proper breathing, relaxation, and emotional controls along with diet and exercise.

But if we aren't sensitive to the feedback and internal control systems, if we lack self-awareness, we can't manage them effectively. Then we have no choice but to depend on medication to maintain a safe blood pressure. Most people don't cure high blood pressure; they simply manage the symptom through medication. When they stop the medication, their blood pressure goes back up.

Lack of self-awareness on a psychological level keeps us enslaved to emotional habits and weaknesses. Worse, we remain unaware of our true strength and powerful mental capabilities, such as instincts and wisdom. Many people believe they aren't creative, yet child-development experts tell us that as high as ninety to ninety-five percent of children tested at age four demonstrate high creative abilities. Yet, within just a few years, the percentages drop to ten to fifteen percent. What happened to the creative abilities? The capacity doesn't disappear; it is buried beneath false negative beliefs such as "I am not creative," or "I'm not worthwhile." For the vast majority, negative self-images remain powerful because they are never examined and resolved through self-knowledge. We literally become slaves to our unexamined habits, and consequently, we are victimized by those who know how to manipulate those habits and beliefs.

The fact that we remain unaware of the vast part of the mind doesn't mean that we must remain so. We can expand our awareness of this unknown part of the mind. We already do so for part of the mind, which we call the sub-conscious mind. The sub-conscious mind consists of those elements of our mind that we typically are not aware of until we direct our attention to them. We are typically unaware of the feelings in the bottom of our left foot until we pay attention to that foot. Until we pay attention, those sensations are part of our sub-conscious mind. However, no matter how hard we try, most of us cannot feel the operation of our spleen. For the vast majority of people, this experience lies totally outside of their awareness in the so-called unconscious mind.

Our culture is so externally oriented that we actually know very little about what happens inside the mind and body. Western science claims that such a phenomenon called mind doesn't even exist, and it certainly doesn't provide the conceptual frameworks and the practical tools necessary to understand the mind. We recognize that emotional intelligence is a crucial factor for success in all aspects of life. But identifying and labeling emotions doesn't provide any awareness of what they are, nor does it give us the power to control and use them effectively.

Confusing Self-Knowledge with Information

Most people, including professionals, confuse self-knowledge with information. Many people have a great deal of information about themselves but very little self-knowledge. In fact, we are buried in information about ourselves. We take psychological tests by the dozens, executives endure "360 degree feedback" and performance evaluations, psychiatrists create huge manuals of diagnostic categories, and marketing companies constantly seek to discover preferences, likes, and dislikes. But all the statistics, labels, and propaganda we hear or read about ourselves add not one whit to self-knowledge.

It may be helpful to know how you compare to others on some personality test, such as the Myers-Briggs, or how your coworkers experience your behavior, but it is not self-knowledge until you consciously experience that behavior within yourself. There is no self-knowledge without inner self-awareness. The best psychological test, the most accurate feedback, the greatest psychologist – cannot provide you with self-knowledge. They can only give you information *about* you. We all have blind spots in our character. Others see an aspect of ourselves, and even confront us on it, but if we don't experience or "see" it, we simply don't accept or believe what they say. If we agree with their insight, and claim to understand, we really don't because we aren't aware of that aspect within ourselves. Even if we change our behavior, we still don't have any understanding. We are simply doing what we are told to do and the change is cosmetic and superficial. Most often, nothing really changes *because we cannot change what we aren't aware of.*

If we use information as a starting point to focus attention inwards, then the psychological test, the 360-degree feedback, or the insights of the great psychologist become useful tools for us as we struggle to gain inner awareness of the characteristics indicated by the information. As we pay attention to our inner realities, we create self-knowledge. As we gain self-knowledge, we gain opportunities to grow, change, or enhance that particular characteristic or quality that was the subject of the external information. But the absolutely necessary key is conscious, direct inner awareness of the characteristic or quality. External information must be verified by internal awareness if it is to be useful at all.

Another common confusion equates self-knowledge with self-analysis. Many people seem to think that if you always analyze yourself, you will eventually understand yourself and rid yourself of these nagging personality issues. Unfortunately, this is not the case. Thoughts, just as physical events, are structured and regulated by the power of habit. In other words, we are consistent not only in what we think, but also how we think. The greatest challenge to self-knowledge is our enormous capacity to fool ourselves. The mind is an ego-bound organization of energy patterns consisting of thoughts, images, emotions, or feelings. Like any organization, the mind employs different means by which to protect itself from pain and maintain its internal structure. Freud called these defense mechanisms, and they are used by the mind to protect it from shame, anxiety, or loss of self-esteem. These defense mechanisms are usually unconscious, which means that we are, for the most part, unaware of what the mind is doing.

When we analyze ourselves, we are using the same instrument that creates the behaviors we are trying to understand. This is like asking the fox to come into the hen house and guard the chickens. What will the mind tell us? It tells us whatever it needs to tell us in order to protect itself and maintain internal consistency. All of which means that it is very easy to deceive ourselves. Consequently, self-analysis is risky and unreliable, and of limited value. It can be used, but used with an extreme dose of skepticism as to the answers that the mind provides.

There is a way that self-analysis can be a useful process. When part of a program of introspection, self-analysis is transformed into a dialogue with the mind. When you dialogue with the mind, you talk with the mind as if you were having an honest, open, and caring conversation with a close friend. In this way, you can have a conversation about anything instead of challenging the mind and running the risk of alerting defense mechanisms. During the dialogue, listen to what your mind says to you. If you respect the mind and treat it gently, it will reveal all its secrets, sooner or later. But the moment you become emotionally disturbed, critical, or judgmental, the mind closes down and operates out of habit. Accurate information becomes increasingly difficult to obtain, and old habits and patterns are reinforced.

Introspection: The Science of Inner Awareness

Self-dialogue is one of the methods used in the scientific methodology of introspection. To introspect means to look within, to be aware of one's thoughts and feelings. Introspection is the systematic expansion of inner awareness for the purpose of self-knowledge. It is a powerful tool for developing inner awareness when employed properly as a rigorous methodology. The great meditative traditions all have rigorous, scientific systems of introspection that lead to ever-increasing levels of self-knowledge. These systems are scientific because they utilize experimental methods and require repetition and verification, which are the defining characteristics of any science. Realizing that the mind has a marvelous capacity to deceive, these traditions are systematic, providing increasing levels of sophisticated methodologies that require increasing levels of discipline. Verification is provided through a number of ways, including repetition, outside resources such as qualified teachers, and written records of experiments done by others. They also provide sophisticated conceptual frameworks necessary to guide and direct efforts.

When western psychology first developed as a distinct discipline, introspection was one of the scientific methods used by early academic psychologists. These efforts were doomed to failure, however, for a number of reasons: the lack of a systematic discipline or methodology, the complete lack of skilled experts to serve as models and provide instruction (the psychologists doing the research had no experience or skills themselves, so it was a classical case of the blind leading the blind), and absolutely no conceptual framework to guide the efforts. Because it was not disciplined, it quickly degenerated into a neurotic self-indulgence that invalidated any results. Western culture still does not have a tradition of disciplined introspection, and that is a great weakness. Moreover, western science makes a limiting assumption, and it is only an assumption based on limited experience, that the brain is the only reality. This is the consequence of a serious defect within western science called objectification. Science intentionally and systematically ignores what the great physicist Erwin Schrodinger called the "Subject of Cognizance" from the domain of inquiry. As Shimon Malin (a Professor of Physics at Colgate University and a leading authority on quantum mechanics) points out in *Nature Loves to Hide,* this results in the disastrous consequence of eliminating values and meaningfulness and the strange impasse in western philosophy of the "mind-body problem."

Western science also lacks rigorous conceptual frameworks or theories that allow for any possibility of a spiritual-Self separate from, and superior to, the brain and its neural activity. Consequently, western sciences, including psychology and psychiatry, have no systematic methodology to objectively study the activities of the mind. After all, if you assume that such a thing as mind doesn't even exist, how can you possibly study it? All you have left is brain activity. Western science has a great deal of information about brain states, and little to no understanding about the human mind. Consequently, for the individual interested in self-knowledge, western science offers very little. Without the ability to become a witness to the mind by experiencing the spiritual-Self, part of the mind ends up observing itself and objective, accurate data is difficult, if not impossible, to attain.

In the meditative traditions, the power of introspection lies in learning to step outside of the ego-self into the spiritual-Self and from that vantage point, observe or witness the on-going activities of mind and body. Now the mind/body complex becomes an object of consciousness, enabling objective knowledge to be obtained through direct experience of the subtle events, processes and patterns in the mind. Introspection is always prone to "subjective" bias as long as you remain locked in the ego-self as personal identity. Only after the mystical experience, when personal identity, the sense of personal I-ness, shifts from the ego-self to the spiritual-Self, do we begin to free ourselves from this bias. Until that identity shift occurs, we must always consider the information we receive from introspection as a tentative possibility, not a definitive reality, and take it along with a large grain of salt.

One of the more important benefits of meditation is this increasing capacity to be a witness to, or an observer of, the mind. Observation is neither a simple nor an easy process. It requires that we focus awareness without any judgment, intention, or investment whatsoever in what we are observing. This is a difficult skill to learn, but it is absolutely necessary if one is to gain valid and reliable information about the mind. This is critical, for the moment we judge something bad or good, the mind reacts by either becoming defensive or providing more of the same. To refrain from judging does not mean that we don't discriminate between cause and effect. The power of discrimination is one of the most important outcomes of observation. A key point in science is the ability to ascertain cause/effect relationships without bias. This is why scientific experiments are carefully arranged to minimize any bias. We must do the same with the mind. The science of introspection requires that we minimize any chance of bias, and when observing the mind, this is a critical element.

Self-knowledge arises naturally from this ability to witness, to observe the on-going activities of the mind. It is this expanded awareness, not analysis, which provides us the knowledge we need to exercise control. It is similar to understanding ice cream. If we were host to an individual from a very "primitive" culture, and they asked us about ice cream, we certainly wouldn't send them to a university class, provide them with chemical analyses, or have them analyze the molecular structure. We would simply have them taste the ice cream. It is in the tasting that we experience and understand ice cream. The same is true with the mind. We need to observe without judgment, without preconceptions, and the mind will reveal itself to us.

As we gain self-knowledge, we gain ability to utilize the subtle and powerful mental resources that were previously hidden from us. The same is true with spiritual realities. The more we gain in Self realization, the greater our use of the spiritual resources available to each and every one of us. The principle of knowledge leads to the second principle, that of will, the creative principle.

Will: The Creative Force

Most of us think of the term "will" as having the determination – the power, persistence, and perseverance – to make something. While this is a small part, the spiritual principle of will is much broader and far more complex. As a spiritual principle, will is the power behind the creative thrust. Before anything can happen, there must be an act of will, a decision to create. Nothing is created out of nothing. Everything has a cause even if the cause itself is unknown. The only exception is God, considered by all religious traditions to be the Uncaused Cause or Primal Mover. But all religions also state that manifest reality is created or emanates, from the will of God. Different religious traditions have different ways of symbolizing or talking about this. But all agree that it is the will of God that brings about material reality. But like other spiritual principles, will applies just as powerfully and appropriately to the mundane level.

Will is the combination of two aspects: intention and desire. Before any action can be engaged, there must be intention to create that action. Intentionality is the underlying expression of intelligence that directs or shapes the creative thrust. Intentionality also involves decisiveness on such a level that there exists no doubt or countervailing tendency.

The power of this thrust is desire. Desire is the unalloyed and unconflicted driving force that brings about an event. If there is only intention, then we are powerless to create anything. And desire without intention is an unfocused blind force, leading only to chaos and havoc. We can understand will as the creative principle of focused energy. As such, will becomes empowered and irresistible. The term for this in tantric philosophy is sankalpa shakti, the power of will.

On a practical and personal level, will is the active, intentional process of creating the reality in which we live. We are actively engaged in creating that reality on a moment-to-moment basis, on all physical, mental, and emotional levels. What we call reality is a construction, not the perception, of a fixed or given reality. Most people believe that what they see is what actually exists. Somehow, the object we experience with our senses is translated into some thought or picture, and there is a one-to-one correspondence between what we think, hear, see, and so forth, is actually there. This belief is called naïve realism.

But scientific research in the biophysics of perception and brain function confirms that what we call reality is a creative dynamic construction built on various and changing neural fields in the brain. When we say that we process information, what we really are saying is that the brain *constructs* information out of an unknown, diverse set of frequency-potentials. What we perceive is the end product of the *construction*, not something that comes in from the outside. That doesn't mean that we create the stone wall, the swallow, the tree in the yard, but that how we see, think about, and relate to that event we call a stone wall, swallow, or tree, is an internal construction. Our personal reality is essentially that: personal. Our collective reality is essentially that: collective. As Joseph Chilton Pierce points out in *Evolutions End,* "Our perceived environment or lived experience is an end-product to which we *ipso facto* attribute the source of that experience. This common-sense, rather inevitable observation is as fundamental an error as attributing the source of the television play to the machine (television set) itself."

This does not mean that material reality only exists in the mind of man. This philosophical position is called subjective idealism, and, like naïve realism, simply has no validity. Those who argue this belief would scarcely do so standing in the path of an on-coming 18-wheeler truck. What the research shows, and what spiritual traditions recognize, is that each of us *constructs* our personal sense of reality. What we relate to is not simply sense data stimulated by what we experience as the rocks, birds, and trees, but an entire construction of meaning. We fit sensory input into an organization of meaning that we construct on a moment-to-moment basis. As Pierce succinctly states further in

Evolutions End, "That the resulting structure of our reality is an internal 'self-organizing' system gives no basis at all, however, for assuming we 'create' that world as it is to itself. Tree and stone in my backyard, bat in our church belfry: Each is its own display, each its own dynamic drawing on, spinning out of, feeding back into the cosmic soup. As physicist Ilya Prigogine observed, 'What ever we call reality, it is revealed to us only through the active construction in which we participate.' The issue is not just a reality, but what is revealed to us."

This construction is the creative process of will. Unfortunately, we are rarely aware of the dynamic exchange going on. Consequently, we are seldom skilled in the use of will, and have very little conscious choice about the realities we create. The more we participate in this construction in a conscious way, the more successful we are at creating the realities we really want instead of suffering from happenstance. And this can occur not only at a personal level, but also at a community, national or even international level. Most successful people understand that they created the conditions for their success. Successful spiritual people, sages and mystics, know that they have created their entire reality. When a great yogic sage states that "I make the sun rise, I make the sun set; all things arise in me," the sage is not claiming miraculous power, but stating what he or she experiences as an obvious fact. The sage understands and consciously experiences will, the dynamic construction of reality.

But where there is little self-awareness and even less self-discipline, we create realities for ourselves that are destructive physically, mentally, and socially. We have all too many examples: politicians who beat the drums of fear and revenge; the media that constantly trumpets the need to be fearful; and fundamentalist religionists (and it doesn't matter what religion, the mentality is the same) who proclaim that God wants us to smite our enemies. (All fundamentalists and politicians claim that God is on their side). This climate of fear and hatred closes down every powerful, positive resource in the human mind as mental control is dominated by ancient reptilian brain functions. The intellect serves, and is dominated by, unthinking, reflexive fight or flight reactions. The consequence is the same as it has been throughout human history: more war, more violence, and more destruction.

Through self-discipline and self-knowledge, we develop the capacity to engage will, our natural ability to respond creatively, powerfully, and with intelligence. Instead of seeing the British as "the enemy," Ghandi included them in his search for truth and freedom. He strongly felt that the British were as much victimized by their imperialism as were the Indian people. This allowed Ghandi to resist without violence because he had no fear or hatred of the English. His desire for freedom, his intentions for truth and non-violence, included all peoples, not just Indian people. Through will, we can live without fear and hatreds, in harmony with ourselves and each other. Ghandi fully expressed his will, responding to challenge with compassion, clarity, focus, and purpose. His mind was free of the fear and hatreds that often characterize leaders of all kinds. Neither Ghandi nor Hitler was an accidental human being, a genetic aberration that happens only by chance. They represent two very different human potentials. We have the capacity for fear, hatred, and violence, but we also have a greater capacity for love, compassion, and creativity. The question is: Do we have the knowledge and will to exercise the latter? Or do we remain stuck in primitive reaction?

Without conscious will, we are left with wishes and wants but have no power to bring them about. For example, we all know what to do, but somehow we lack the determination to do what we already know we should. In other words, we know what to do but we don't know how to be. How many times do we wish that things were different, that we didn't have to worry so much, that we had leaders who were wise and principled, or that we could live in peace and harmony? We have all the good intentions, but without the conscious exercise of will, these intentions fall by the wayside. We often let fears and concerns interfere with our will, and we delay making a decision, doing what we already know is necessary, or avoid finishing a project, even though in our heart of hearts, we know what to do. The lack of developing and using a powerful will, or *sankalpa shakti,* is the source of a great many problems.

Through self-knowledge and self-discipline, the warrior sage develops will as a conscious tool, using his power of intention and desire to skillfully create realities that benefit others. He understands that the way he sees reality is nothing more than a construction, and he has the freedom – the skill and knowledge – necessary to create the realities that are helpful to himself and others. Like Ghandi, he moves in the world with compassion and effectiveness, taking actions that benefit the world rather than harm the world. This is called "skillful action," and reflects the third spiritual principle, action.

Action: Power of Transformation

Action is the principle of transformation, of change. Life is not static; to be alive means to engage change, and the agent of change is action. Knowledge is not gained and will is not expressed until action is taken. Without action, focused desire, or will, leads only to impotency. But just as knowledge and will are constants, action is also a constant. It is an inseparable part of the reality around us. Only God is free from action, yet only through action does God express, create, or manifest the reality in which we live.

As a spiritual principle, action means *skillful action,* not just any and all actions. Skillful action is action that brings about greater balance and harmony rather than imbalance and disharmony. This isn't "right" (as opposed to "wrong") action, but action that is in harmony with the reality within which it is embedded. It is action free of egoism and the negative conditions and motivations of the mind. Skillful action is characterized by at least four distinct qualities: non-attachment, ease, insight, and spontaneity.

Essential to skillful action is non-attachment, the freedom from ownership. Non-attachment does not mean non-involved, it means not depending on any one or several things for a sense of security, fulfillment, happiness, or contentment. It is freedom from the compulsion of driving needs and wants. Non-attachment allows us to use all of the things of the world without having to own any of them. It is non-attachment that allows us to be selfless, to be open to change, to allow the hidden forces to emerge and be known. It allows us to accept other beliefs, share power, and allow others to express themselves without feeling that we are wrong, unimportant, or less than someone else. Simply speaking, whatever we "own" in our mind owns us back, and becomes a potential source for emotional disturbances. As we will see later, we must learn non-attachment to successfully develop the spiritual discipline of prayer.

A mind at ease is free from negative emotions, such as greed, lust for power, name and fame, anger, and fear. Emotional disturbances create a reactive mind, making responding much more difficult and erratic. The source of ease is emotional integrity, the discipline and knowledge to access and effectively manage the resources of the mind. We create stress when we mismanage these resources, and stress leads to actions that are not only ineffective, but also destructive on many levels. When thoughts and actions are forced, ease is lost and resistances are created. Under pressure, mistakes are made and flexibility is lost. When flexibility is lost, strength becomes brittle and actions become desperate. Without ease, there is great danger in all actions.

With insight, beginnings are easily recognized, and directions on how to proceed become obvious. Insight arises from knowledge, perceptual clarity, and inner harmony. It is the result of a penetrating awareness created by a calm, clear, mind attentively attuned to the present and emerging realities in which it exists. Calmness brings clarity and simplicity to the most complex of events. With an uncluttered mind, we refine attention and perceive events more clearly, tuning into subtle cause/effect relationships generally ignored by most people.

Spontaneous action is action unrestricted by habit. It is responsive action, guided by reflective awareness, intention, and thought rather than habitual reaction, which serves egocentric needs and fears. Spontaneity arises from an inner harmony that induces effortlessness, and a perceptual sensitivity attuned to the subtle realities that lead to effective, timely actions. Spontaneous action is not chaotic, but focused and appropriate to the demands of the situation. Actions become potent when they are responses to the here and now. Spontaneous actions are without calculation, without manipulation, without hidden agendas. They are clean and clear, effective in the moment even though the results may not be known for some time.

Skillful action is effortless action because it arises out of harmony, is expressed in harmony, and ends in harmony. Skillful action is both obvious and compelling. It is the right action at the right time in the right place. In action, timing is everything. That doesn't mean skillful action is always pleasurable or pain-free, only that it is an action that comes from inner strength and harmony and leads to greater harmony and success.

On an individual level, action is the foundation of self-discipline, or the building of conscious skills. Without effort, nothing is achieved. This is the practical meaning of "As ye sow, so shall ye reap." This biblical phrase is not about sin or judgment of any kind, but the clear recognition of the spiritual principle of action, and the consequences of skilled or unskilled action. The warrior sage understands that sustained, skilled, and systematic effort must be made if great wisdom, acts, and outcomes are to be achieved. Skill only comes from disciplined practice. Just as it takes great practice to create a skilled Olympic athlete, it takes even greater practice to achieve Olympian strength, wisdom, and skill. It is not simply practicing different exercises, but a lifetime commitment to personal excellence, costing not less than everything.

These three universal spiritual principles – knowledge, will and action – are essential to both self-mastery and Self realization. They constitute the essential elements of response ability, an essential quality of the warrior sage. The journey of Self realization and self-mastery is synergistic. The same disciplines that lead to the qualities of the sage also build the qualities of the warrior.

Realization, Mastery and Personal Response Ability

Unlike most leaders, political or otherwise, Gandhi did not want to control or rule over others, he strove to have people control themselves. This was the essence of his principle of swaraj, rule over one's own. He realized that only when people became courageous and confronted their fears, hatreds, and prejudices, only when they achieved self-mastery, would they achieve and sustain real political freedom. The historical lessons are quite clear. How many times have ego-driven revolutionaries turned into dictators? How many times have certain groups claimed political freedom only to enslave those who were not in the right group, or those who were powerless? How often does money and power, the aphrodisiacs of the ego-self, determine policy rather than truth, compassion, and service to others?

The warrior sage does not conquer others; he conquers the destructive forces within himself. Spiritual-Self realization and ego-self mastery are accomplished through personal responsibility. This is not some strange eastern concept. All religions speak about the necessity for self-responsibility. It was a central concept for both Socrates and Plato. Found in the writings of Thomas Jefferson, Benjamin Franklin, and other founders of the American Constitution, personal responsibility forms the cornerstone of the American Democratic Republic where the American citizen is, by constitutional law, the sole source of governmental power, not some powerful elite, a political party, or a religious ideology.

Sadly, Americans have abdicated much of their personal responsibilities to political parties and ruling elites. The "land of the free and the home of the brave" is fast becoming the land of the over-regulated and controlled, and the home of the fearful. We are exchanging our freedom for the illusion of safety. The great philosophers of all ages recognize that genuine freedom, whether it is political, economic, or personal, can only be achieved through personal responsibility.

The term "responsibility" can have several meanings. For instance, we often use it as a way to accuse someone of a mistake: "You are responsible for this mess!" At other times it indicates a burden placed on our backs by someone else. In the context of the warrior sage, the term "responsibility" actually means something quite different. If we break the word into its component parts, we find two words: "response" and "ability." It actually refers to the ability to respond to a particular situation.

Most of us react to situations rather than respond to the best of our ability. What personal responsibility is all about is the ability to respond effectively to situations, to make choices rather than react out of habits and emotions. Gandhi's principle of swaraj means the ability to respond skillfully, rather than be driven by habits, fears, greed, stress, and all the other powerful emotional pressures that often dominate thoughts and actions.

Swaraj: Living With Strategic Intelligence

Strategic intelligence is a broad concept that involves the practical application of the three spiritual principles of knowledge, will and action. Strategic intelligence is the ability to skillfully use the inner resources of the mind and body for optimal performance and personal fulfillment. Through it, we achieve true personal response ability. We respond to challenge with clarity, creativity, and balance; work with vision, confidence, and enthusiasm; and act with integrity, commitment, and compassion. In other words, strategic intelligence allows us to become the skillful human being that defines the warrior sage.

We are born with all the resources we need, but that doesn't guarantee strategic intelligence. We develop strategic intelligence skills through self-training: accessing, developing, and enhancing all the human resources contained within the body, mind, and spirit. Simultaneously we build the strength and clarity needed to transcend self-mastery and achieve spiritual-Self realization. Through the spiritual disciplines of prayer, meditation, and contemplation, we unlock the powerful resources of the sage and establish our identity with the spiritual-Self. We now experience the power and clarity of the warrior along with the wisdom, compassion and tranquility of the sage. All this occurs naturally as a process of growth and evolution as we use the inner technologies of the spiritual traditions to guide the unfolding of our human potential.

We are unique human beings, each with different capacities, but each of us has the obligation to ourselves and to our common humanity to become whole. This is what self-mastery and spiritual-Self realization is all about – fulfilling human potential. To accomplish this, we have two powerful instruments of tools: the mind and the body. By taking command of these two instruments, we become fully qualified warriors. As we develop these capacities for balance, strength and strategic intelligence, we complete the difficult journey to become a sage. It is a journey as fascinating as it is rewarding. Each step brings us closer to our destiny of the warrior sage. In the next chapter, we will briefly review the tools and techniques necessary to unlock these inner capacities.

Chapter Four
Tools of the Trade

Human intelligence, and the skill to use that intelligence,
is the fundamental resource of each and every one of us.
—Phil Nuernberger—

Look around. The building you are in, the beliefs, thoughts, and emotions you have, the life you have created, the reality you experience are all created by this powerful instrument we call the human mind. Culture, history, achievements, governments, religions are all created by the human mind. The human mind is the instrument we use to form knowledge, all knowledge! Everything – thoughts, actions, strategies, plans, empires – is created, involves, and passes through this amazing instrument. Yet, most of us have not even the faintest idea how the mind works or understand the creative power of this incredible instrument. Even those who study it seem to be befuddled, or worse, preoccupied with its pathologies. Sigmund Freud, arguably the world's most famous psychiatrist, could only see the pathology and sickness that occupies a small fraction of the mind, and remained ignorant of the vast creative power, domains of knowledge, complexity, and beauty of the total mind.

It's clear that we tap only a very small percentage of the creative power of the mind. Even Einstein once estimated that he used only about ten percent of his true capabilities. If Einstein was correct, where does that leave the rest of us? Most of us develop a few abilities to some degree, and some of us develop one or two to a very high degree of proficiency. But for the most part, we remain incomplete human beings, using only a small percentage of our true potential. And the reason is deceptively simple: we are ignorant of the power that lies beyond our normal awareness. Ignorance does not mean that we are dumb, or that we lack education. Ignorance means exactly what it says: to ignore, to be unaware, to be unconscious.

Not only are we unaware of the subtle and powerful resources and control systems of the mind and body, many even doubt that they exist. As discussed earlier, most of the western scientific community doesn't even believe that any such phenomenon as the human mind even exists. The consequence of this assumption is that we labor under remarkably primitive conceptual frameworks concerning thought, consciousness, and mind.

It isn't surprising that we don't know how to access and develop our mental powers as conscious skills. Our education is incomplete, limited to beliefs and systems that prevent us from accessing and utilizing our full potential. Trapped by our ignorance, we continue to create problem after problem, only vaguely aware of the powerful resources for inner strength, success, joy, and personal fulfillment that lie hidden beneath the surface of our habits and beliefs.

The human mind is enormously creative and powerful. But we lack the self-knowledge and self-discipline necessary to develop and use these powerful inner resources as conscious tools. Consequently, we function at a small percentage of our true capacity, remaining enslaved by habits we do not consciously choose. Some use a few resources to create material wealth, but then live in emotional, intellectual, and spiritual poverty. As Henry David Thoreau remarked, most people live "lives of quiet desperation," and these lives are characterized by stress created by fears, frustrations, and negativity. Ask yourself how many truly contented, joyful, fulfilled individuals do you know and work with?

Recognizing this, the warrior sage engages in a systematic process, a discipline, specifically designed to access, develop, and use his inner strengths and resources. He understands that personal greatness is the expression of one's total being, not a consequence of style or intellectual knowledge. His quest is to realize the full power of the personality and the human spirit, and bring their enormous strategic resources into conscious use. This isn't an easy task, particularly in a modern culture that places so much emphasis on material signs of power and accomplishment, and where educational systems often create obstacles to self-awareness and self-discipline.

Spiritual-Self realization provides the foundation of personal greatness. But the expression of the spiritual-Self depends on the ego-self, the mind/body complex with all its strategic resources. The task is to tap the subtle and powerful spiritual resources and express them skillfully through the two instruments of the mind and body. This requires that we create a healthy ego-self where the strategic resources of the mind and body serve the spiritual-Self. This is called self-mastery. Self-mastery is not a matter of reading books, getting a college degree, or attending seminars. It is exactly what the term indicates: mastery of the ego-self and the resources of the mind and body.

This journey of spiritual, mental, and physical fulfillment demands a systematic discipline, a powerful spiritual tradition that provides not only the concepts, but also the practical tools and techniques that lead both to Self realization and self-mastery. It requires access to, and guidance from, accomplished mentors within a tradition, individuals who have taken the journey, who know the subtle pathways to personal fulfillment, and whose only interest is in leading others to Self realization and independence.

Again, this is not to say that there is only one way to get to the pinnacle. Each individual must discover his or her own path, and this path necessarily reflects the uniqueness of the individual ego-self. Human beings are open systems, and capable of arriving at the same end through a variety of ways.

Beliefs, concepts, and practices vary from culture to culture, time to time, and tradition to tradition. But, as we saw in the last chapter, underlying these differences are universal processes and principles that are the same regardless of the particular spiritual tradition. These constitute the foundation of every spiritual and self-mastery tradition.

For example, Zen meditation exercises are somewhat different than Kabalistic meditation exercises. However, both lead to increased insight and wisdom. The exercises or techniques are particular, but the use of meditation for inner balance, increased energy and power, greater emotional control, and deep insight, is universal. Christian beliefs and practices differ from Jewish and Muslim beliefs and practices, but both are ways to celebrate spiritual experience and knowledge. They have different ways of worshipping, understanding, and experiencing the divine. But these traditions utilize the same underlying universal spiritual practices and the same underlying ego-self practices involving the body, energy, and mind.

Starting From a Core Tradition

While traditions differ, they play a crucial role in the development of a warrior sage. A tradition is an established body of knowledge, beliefs, and practices. There are many kinds – academic, scientific, religious, even martial traditions, to name just a few. Few traditions, however, are sophisticated or sufficiently deep enough to provide the comprehensive inner technology necessary to develop the warrior sage.

For example, most established religions offer little in training the various powers and levels of the human mind and body. They are far more concerned with telling their followers what to do than providing the practical methodologies necessary to give individuals the resources they need to make their own decisions.

This is a great weakness of many religions and philosophies. They tell us what we *should do*, but offer little in the way of *how to be*. As a consequence, religions tend to be authoritarian, creating a priest class which places itself as mediator between the individual and the divine. This systemic weakness of religions robs the individual believer of personal response ability and power, and greatly inhibits individual spiritual and personal growth.

Science, likewise, has a number of traditions, but none of them provide the knowledge or tools necessary for self-management, nor do they offer anything useful for the study of consciousness and the spiritual dimension. Western science is narrowly focused on material phenomenon, and as Schrodinger and Malin* point out, systematically excludes the subjective aspect of reality. Yet, the reality is that all scientific data means nothing until the individual mind makes sense (creates meaning) out of it. This is not to say that science is wrong, only that it has a very focused and limited perspective.

Our concern here is with spiritual traditions that recognize the transcendent nature of human beings, and offer wholistic disciplines that encompass both the spiritual dimension as well as the mind/body material dimension. These wholistic traditions of spiritual humanism embrace knowledge derived from all valid traditions – philosophical, scientific, social, religious – whatever contributes to greater understanding of the human condition.

Spiritual traditions encompass a variety of approaches and activities that focus on enhancing self-knowledge and self-discipline. They necessarily differ in philosophy, focus, methods, and techniques. These differences reflect the incredible variety and openness of the human system. The goal of spiritual-Self realization, however, does not differ. While many claim that their tradition is the best path, and all too often, arrogantly claim that it is the only path, these claims concerning superiority hold very little relationship to truth. As we stated earlier, there is a superior path for each individual, but it is the path that suits that particular individual. It is each individual's sole responsibility to explore, experiment, and discover which tradition fits his or her own unique needs, and will support his or her quest for becoming a warrior sage.

While many of the differences between the great spiritual traditions are cultural in nature, there are factors that differentiate traditions and play a crucial role in developing the warrior sage. These factors include:

• an emphasis on independent personal response ability. Warrior sage traditions are not interested in creating followers, but rather in developing responsible independence and self-rule (Gandhi's concept of *swaraj*), along with respect and acceptance of the great diversity of the human experience;

---

* *Nature Loves to Hide: Quantum Physics and the Nature of Realilty, A Western Perspetive.* Shimon Malin, Oxford University Press, 2001.

• a high degree of wholism which address all aspects of human experience – physical, mental/emotional, spiritual, social, ethical;

• sophisticated, reliable and effective inner technologies that provide practical methods and tools necessary to become skilled in both spiritual skills and the strategic skills of the mind;

• an emphasis on direct experience as the foundation of knowledge, experimentation, and self-discovery rather than the blind acceptance of doctrine, with faith built on direct experience rather than blind faith in the words written in some sacred text.

Building the powerful structure of the warrior sage demands a solid foundation. It is crucial that each individual discover a core tradition, and develop an in-depth knowledge and skill within that chosen system. As we gain depth in knowledge and skill in a particular spiritual tradition, we gain greater insight into all others. As we build this foundation, we are able to explore and learn from all other traditions. And given the great variety of human interests and innate capacities, we necessarily engage more than one tradition to expand our capacity, knowledge and understanding. But if we jump from one discipline to another without establishing a solid foundation in a core spiritual tradition, our knowledge remains limited and superficial.

For example, the author's tradition is tantra yoga, which was a natural evolution of my training in classical ashtanga yoga. (The word *ashtanga*, meaning "eight limbs," is based on the *Yoga Sutras* by Patanjali.) Although my training included hatha yoga, my interests in physical training lie in the martial arts. At the suggestion of my tantric yoga master, I began formal training in Washin Ryu Karate, but eventually moved to Shaolin Taijichuen, and studied Taoism, which I see as closely related to tantra. I am also fascinated by quantum physics and its implications for brain function, mind, and consciousness. These different traditions serve to enrich my tantric practices and philosophy. Swami Jaidev, a vedic swami of the Bharati Order, is a close friend who shares my tantric tradition. He is an American of Irish descent, has doctorates in theology and philosophty, teaches meditation and hatha yoga, and is a practitioner in a Japanese martial art. Like myself, his studies in other traditions (theology, Akido, and Vedanta philosophy) all support his core tradition of tantra yoga. The key is to build diversity of knowledge on a firm foundation of discipline and direct experience.

Body, Mind, and Spirit

For the warrior sage, learning is an expanding and synergistic process, integrating techniques and principles from other traditions into the core tradition. The goal is the integration of the powerful resources of body, mind, and spirit through a variety of physical, mental, and spiritual practices. Becoming a warrior sage demands systematic development utilizing a variety of techniques and tools. Figure 4:1 on the following page is a diagram of this synergistic process. Between the powerful principles that define the spiritual and material foundation and the achievement of the warrior sage are the inner disciplines, the spiritual pathways and the inner technologies of the mind/body complex. These inner disciplines constitute the core of every great spiritual tradition. They provide the leverage necessary to bring about the skills of personal and leadership greatness.

If all we have is an intellectual understanding of our spiritual, mental, and physical resources, they remain only theoretical possibilities. The great spiritual traditions provide not only well-defined pathways of prayer, meditation and contemplation; they also include sophisticated methods of ego-self mastery as well. These are the tools of the trade, so to speak, the proven inner technologies of personal growth and transformation. The inner technologies of the ego-self not only lead to skilled use of the mind/body complex, but also provide essential support for spiritual-Self realization.

We live life as a total human being, simultaneously living and working on several planes or dimensions. If we remain undeveloped and unskilled in some aspects of life, these create problems that impact other areas of life. How we handle diet and exercise impact emotional and intellectual abilities, just as emotions influence the digestive tract, the immune system, and even the muscles. Depending on how we act towards others will either create harmony – in the team, in the family, or between cultures – or create discord, hostility, and even warfare. We can live with stress and the myriads of problems that it brings, or we can live in harmony and contentment. There are always choice points where success is determined by levels of skill. We abdicate any choice when we do not have the inner disciplines of ego-self mastery and the spiritual skills of spiritual-Self realization. Let's briefly examine the various disciplines and their purpose for the warrior sage.

Figure 4:1

Inner Technologies of Ego-self Mastery

Balance/Energy Disciplines for flexiblilty, balance, emotional integrity, strength

Focusing Disciplines to develop awareness, concentration, genuine self-confidence

Strategic Disciplines for creativity, instinct, vision, enhanced problem solving skills

Philosophical/Ethical/Social Disciplines for vital relationships, teamwork, personal fulfillment, harmonious culture

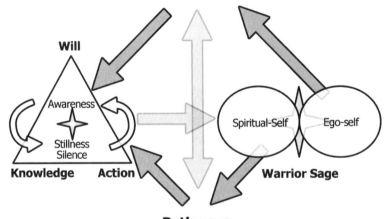

Pathways to Self-Realization (Spiritual Awareness)

Prayer
Meditation
Contemplation

The Inner Technologies of Ego-Self Mastery

We begin with the inner technologies that lead to mastery of the mind/body complex and the ego-self. With these disciplines, we develop the powerful inner resources of the mind and body as conscious skills. Although these inner technologies are listed as separate, this is only for the sake of discussion and clarity. They are interrelated, and involve both the mind and body. For instance, traditional martial arts are profoundly mental disciplines, demanding the development and use of energy, even though physical exercises are the focal point. Likewise, the same practices that lead to balance and emotional integrity also provide the foundation for the strategic disciplines. Focusing disciplines, so necessary for the strategic skills of the mind, also lead to deep physical and mental harmony.

In working with the mind/body complex, the warrior sage is concerned with developing and integrating four essential qualities: balance, power, strategy (application) and fulfillment (success). To accomplish this, he utilizes various disciplines to access the innate resources of the mind and body and turn these resources into conscious skills. It is not a process of becoming different, but of actualizing the power and resources that already exist within the mind/body complex. In other words, using the inner technologies of ego-self mastery, the warrior sage becomes a skilled human being.

Inner Balance as Foundation: Balance/Energy Disciplines

Every great structure needs a solid foundation. The warrior sage systematically creates a body and mind that are healthy, and free from chronic stress and tensions that so often lead to disease. This is far more than fitness training, or reducing fats in the diet. While diet, aerobics, and strength building exercises play an important role, balance and energy disciplines are designed to enhance the inner awareness of the control mechanisms of the mind and body, and lead to greater conscious control over them. These sophisticated disciplines lead to the harmonious integration of mind and body necessary to achieve high levels of wellness and emotional integrity. The warrior sage recognizes the underlying unity of the mind and body, and the energy connection between the two, and consciously uses that profound connection to live without stress, tension, and disease.

The body is both a tool for self-expression, and a powerful tool for training the mind. The warrior sage uses the body to develop the mind. For example, hatha yoga is a sophisticated discipline for using the body to awaken deeper levels of inner awareness. However, most yoga classes as taught in the west – with a growing emphasis on power yoga, yoga olympics, the various name-branding and even trade-marking of postures and language – are nothing more than physical exercises and misrepresent the purpose of hatha yoga. The warrior sage knows the subtle and irrevocable connection between mind and body, and uses the body purposefully to train the mind and open pathways to spiritual-Self awareness.

The great meditative traditions, particularly eastern traditions, acknowledge this connecting link between the mind and body while providing a variety of tools and methods to develop, enhance, and regulate it. These energy disciplines and techniques, such as diaphragmatic breathing, 2:1 breathing and bellows breathing in yoga or Taoist breathing in Taijichuan, lead to greater energy, deeper balance and inner harmony, and enhanced power. Breath is a key component in all great martial arts traditions as well as the meditative traditions. Breath isn't the goal, however; it is simply the tool. The goal of these traditions is the conscious awareness of, and control over, the subtle energy force that is carried by the breath.

This life force energy goes by different names – *prana* in yoga; *chi* in Chinese philosophy, medicine, and martial arts; and *ki* in Japanese traditions. This important dimension of human life has been completely overlooked by western science, which is just now beginning to explore human energy dynamics, largely due to the impact of Chinese medicine and acupuncture.

Flexibility training is another common thread throughout the meditative traditions, as well as a significant part of energy training. Energy practitioners recognize that unnecessary and chronic muscle tension blocks the flow of energy, and leads to imbalanced, stagnant, and unhealthy energy patterns, which in turn, lead to stress, disease, and impaired mental functioning. Again, the focus is on enhancing the mind, not simply making the body strong and healthy. On the other hand, if you can't control your thinking, or mind chatter, you constantly create emotional reactions that lead to chronic stress and tension in the body, reducing flexibility and balance. The warrior sage understands that he alone is the source of his stress, that no one can disturb him unless he first disturbs himself. Through energy/balance disciplines, he learns to direct both the autonomic nervous system and his conscious thoughts, thus eliminating stress from both his mind and body.

Energy/balance disciplines can be as simple and direct as diaphragmatic breathing and breath awareness (simply feeling the breath at the base of the bridge of the nose) which establish neurological harmony and control of mind chatter to eliminate stress. They may also be complex breathing/movement/attentional exercises such as hatha yoga and qigong exercises. But all are designed to increase or enhance:

- over-all wellness, particularly respiratory efficiency and coronary health;
- energy and strength;
- conscious neurological control;
- flexibility, relaxation, and balance;
- emotional stability and control (emotional integrity);
- access to spiritual-Self awareness.

Living with Power: Focusing/Concentration Skills

Life is not meant for weakness. Along with balance, the warrior sage develops the inherent power of the mind. Those who say that knowledge (or information) is power are mistaken. The real power of the mind lies in its ability to focus attention. Of all the different resources and skills that we bring to any task, none are as critical as the ability to focus attention. Think of all the personal skills that you bring to your work, and that allow you to work effectively. You can probably name several: communication skills, creativity, humor, knowledge, management skills, problem-solving skills. The list can be very large indeed. But regardless of how skillful you are, the day you cannot pay attention, these resources and skills will not work.

Success in anything we do depends first and foremost on the ability to focus attention. Literally, the strength of the neural field(s) we create in the brain depends directly, and almost singularly, on our ability to concentrate. Yet we understand little about attention and concentration. Worse, most of us have never had any concentration training as part of our education. With its denial of the mind as a reality, modern science has little to say about the nature of attention and concentration. We must turn to the meditative traditions, which not only have the sophisticated conceptual frameworks that allow us to understand attention and concentration, but also provide sophisticated methods to develop and enhance focusing and concentration abilities.

The great meditative traditions understand the mind to be a field of energy. This allows for a sophisticated understanding and development of concentration. For example, the sixth limb of the eight limbs of astanga yoga is dharana, or concentration. Yoga science provides a number of methods for developing the power of concentration, such as trataka (gaze), breathing practices, and different meditation practices. As we will see later, meditation itself is actually refined concentration, and is the most sophisticated concentration practice available.

The warrior sage recognizes that her finest instrument is the mind, and the most powerful mind is accomplished through concentration. Through practice and discipline, she takes the subtle, and often scattered and relatively weak energy of the mind, and turns it into a powerful beam. Just as light becomes powerful when its photons are synchronized into a laser beam, the mind's energy, when synchronized and focused through the practice of concentration and meditation, becomes laser-like in its power to penetrate any knowledge field. All the natural innate resources of the mind are accessed and enhanced by the synchronization and strengthening of neural fields through concentration and meditation.

The ability to pay attention is a crucial aspect in all forms of knowledge, but it is particularly necessary for the first of three knowledge states of the mind, critical thinking. This knowledge state requires not only clarity of thought, but also the ability to penetrate knowledge fields both in depth and in breadth. Clarity of thought demands that emotional energy be effectively channeled in order to sustain the powerful motivational energy necessary for sustained effort, and at the same time eliminate the bias that most often colors and distorts critical thinking. Knowledge and information by themselves are useless, but when acquired by a disciplined, focused mind, they become powerful tools for both success and fulfillment.

To take command of life demands great self-confidence as well as a powerful will. Without refined skills in concentration, the central core of unlimited self-confidence found in the peaceful center of the mind, remains unknown and untapped, and human will is left weak and powerless. The power to focus attention is crucial to every human endeavor, and is a necessary accomplishment in ego-self mastery for the warrior sage. But the most important of these crucial abilities is the enhanced awareness of the spiritual-Self, which is the natural outcome of meditation.

The Application of Power: Strategic Intelligence Skills

Once she builds the foundation of mental and physical health and balance, making the mind powerful through concentration, the warrior sage is in a strong position to develop and utilize the strategic resources of the mind and body, and to access the wisdom of the spiritual-Self. These resources are perceptual sensitivity, creativity, and the knowledge states of critical thinking, instinct, and intuition. The first of these resources, enhanced perceptual sensitivity plays a central role in nearly all inner resources. The body is like a powerful receiver, tuned to the external world through the five senses. As such, the body is an unparalleled source of information. Through disciplines, such as push hands in Taijichuan and the yoga practice of breath awareness, the warrior sage develops a highly refined awareness of sensory data, hearing what others never hear, seeing details that others don't see, and sensing emotional currents that are often largely overlooked by the untrained mind. This refined sensory ability leads to extraordinary communication skills and sensitivity to environmental subtleties that underlie all successful effort. With enhanced perceptual sensitivity, the warrior sage leader hears the unspoken messages of those she leads, and moves in harmony with underlying currents, avoiding dangers, dead-ends, and unnecessary conflicts.

The body, which is always fully attuned to the entire mind, also reflects unconscious knowledge states, providing another avenue of insight into the thoughts and feelings of others, as well as the subtle insights of the warrior sage's own mind. Developing enhanced awareness of inner realities provides enormous advantages to the warrior sage, allowing for even greater clarity of mind. Awareness of the perceptual process opens the door for creativity, the flexibility to alter perceptual fields, and the ability to think outside of the box. Awareness of perceptual and intellectual habits allows us to step away from habitual ways of being in the world, and create new ways of being. This enhanced ability is the essence of creativity.

More importantly, with enhanced perceptual sensitivity, the warrior sage establishes the foundation for a highly refined instinctual ability, the second of the knowledge states of the mind. Instinct is hardwired, allowing us (and all animals) to move effectively through dangers, know when to advance and when to retreat, and recognize who to trust and who to keep at a distance. This is not an intellectual or logical process of the mind, but a perceptual sensitivity to "what is" in the environment. Instinct alerts us to whatever is in our environment that is either helpful or hurtful. Advanced martial artists, for example, are skilled in recognizing the intent and direction of an attack before their opponent even begins to move their body. Instinct provides the feeling we experience when we walk into a room and the "tension is so thick that you can cut it with a knife." It is that gut feeling that something is not quite right with the situation we are in, or the same way we know that something has happened to our children when they are not even near.

We are instinctual about our children, but typically not for the neighbor's child. This is because instinct is strongest for those for whom we have a loving concern. This loving concern draws our attention, and through attention we become more aware of the subtle realities. The accomplished warrior sage develops the same loving concern for all, as well as an expanded capacity to pay attention. Consequently, he has a refined instinctual ability for all those with whom he relates. On the other hand, the more self-centered we are because of fear, desires, or egoism, the more limited our instinctual knowledge becomes. We feel instinctual knowledge just as we feel our emotions since they both come through the same perceptual channels. Thus, it takes discipline and practice to discern the subtle differences between emotions such as fear and desire, and true instinctual knowledge.

The third knowledge state, intuition, is the most powerful knowledge state of the mind. Intuition is not sensory-based knowledge, but rather arises out of the powerful discriminatory function of the mind. Intuition is based on our ability to discern or discriminate subtle cause/effect relationships that are not limited by the time/space or pleasure/pain restrictions associated with sensory input. That means that intuitive knowledge is not subject to the restrictive limits of habituation, nor the powerful distorting influence of emotions. Intuition tells us the truth about what is, not what we have learned to see, or what our emotions would have us see. We don't feel intuition; it comes as a quiet voice pointing to the truth, a flash of insight, or a simple, calm knowing what is right.

The warrior sage understands intuition to be not only visionary power and the genuine conscience, but also the seat of wisdom. While the power of discrimination is a resource of the mind, the origin of the wisdom lies in the spiritual-Self. When the warrior sage directs his power of discrimination towards the external world, he becomes aware of the unfoldment of future events by the clear discrimination of the subtle cause/effect relationships that exist in the present. When that power is directed inwards, he becomes aware of the wisdom of the spiritual-Self, and when refined, leads to direct awareness of the spiritual-Self.

The warrior sage recognizes the mind to be his finest instrument available. Through inner balance, refined attention, and concentration, and the systematic development of his strategic inner resources, he now has full use of the unique power of the ego-self, the mind/body complex. But personal greatness requires more than just a powerful mind. This power must be directed in ways that lead to personal fulfillment and spiritual realization. A final set of disciplines must also be mastered, and these are the ones that determine purpose.

Human Fulfillment: Philosophical/Ethical/Social Disciplines

Fully aware of the dangers to the ego-self from the acquisition of power, the warrior sage realizes that the greatest dangers he faces are within. They are the inner dragons of his ego: anger; fear; self-hatred; greed for power, wealth, and status; and the lust for pleasure. If the enormous power of the mind, with all its strategic resources, is not directed properly, the result is not personal or leadership greatness, but ego dominated disaster. As we saw earlier, Hitler is a classic example of what can happen when ego-driven leaders come into power.

The warrior sage is careful to develop a personal philosophy, a guiding set of principles that support a singular purpose to life. Like Gandhi, he is unyielding in his commitment to his principles. This personal philosophy is not left to chance, but is systematically developed through reflection and reasoning, an on-going search for truth (as opposed to knowing or having the truth), a constant dedication to freedom, and a mind open to new possibilities, change, and diversity. These principles are derived from a variety of resources: life experiences, intellectual reasoning, and direct spiritual experiences.

The warrior sage accepts nothing on the basis of belief, but systematically explores within himself to find the guiding principles of his own spiritual-Self. He tests all beliefs against his spiritual knowledge and his direct experience. As a consequence, his philosophy is uniquely his own, unshakable and solid in the face of adversity, challenge, or temptation. At the pinnacle of this personal philosophy is the overriding purpose of one's life. It is this purpose that gives direction to action, brings order and simplicity out of chaos and complexity, and provides the stabilizing force in times of change and challenge.

Gandhi's singular purpose in life was the search for truth. This purpose gave direction to his actions and decisions, and served as a bulwark during his struggles for India's independence from England. His efforts were dictated by his purpose, and this gave him the strength to persevere in the face of violence without resorting to violence himself. The warrior sage, like Gandhi, lives a life governed by principle, and given focus by his purpose.

There are specific disciplines that lead to the development of a personal philosophy. Chief among them are the spiritual disciplines discussed in the next chapter. But there are also guiding principles that are found in all great religious, philosophical, and meditative traditions. These principles, such as non-violence, truthfulness, service, and non-possessiveness, are actually practices engaged in by the warrior sage in order to claim them as living principles. For example, truthfulness is a principle, but the practice of truthfulness is a discipline. Nonviolence is a principle, but the practice of not harming in thought, word, and deed is a great discipline. Loving all and excluding none is a great principle, but the practice of selfless service without prejudice is a great discipline.

As the warrior sage engages the disciplines involved in the principles, and continues to grow in spiritual knowledge and inner strength, his ego-self becomes healthy and strong. His relationships become vital, characterized by love and compassion. His personality, tempered by the disciplines he engages, becomes brilliant in its expression. But the great strength that springs forth has its source in the spiritual core, and is the result of the spiritual disciplines that are the counterweight to the immense power of the mind. It is the practice of these spiritual disciplines that bring the individual being into alignment with the universal principles expressed in all great meditative traditions, as well as the great philosophical and religious traditions. It is to these spiritual disciplines that we now turn.

Chapter Five
Prayer – Pathway of the Heart

*. . .then one realizes that life itself is a sort of worship
that can shine on the altar of infinity.*
—His Holiness Swami Rama—

The simplest and most widely traveled spiritual path is prayer. Used in all religions, prayer is a familiar practice to nearly everyone. We hear and participate in prayers in places of worship, at meals, at public gatherings, and even on TV, where nearly everyone from the blow-dried TV evangelist claiming to talk with God while pumping the audience for money, to politicians using prayer as a political issue, to football players who kneel in prayer after scoring a touchdown. It seems that all you have to do is create an audience, and someone is going to pray for something.

We pray for just about everything – for death and destruction to our enemies and victory in battle as well as for peace, for material wealth and power, for health and well-being for ourselves and others, and even, occasionally, for wisdom, strength and enlightenment. One would think that for all the prayers that are said, there would be no war, "my" team would always win, no one would die, and everyone would have great material wealth, happiness, and contentment. Perhaps the problem is that there are too many competing prayers. After all, which prayer on which side of the conflict does God favor? Which side – Republican or Democrat, Israel or Palestine, Catholic or Protestant, Christian or Muslim, Buddhist or Hindu, black or white, my team or yours – should the divine support? And who should have all those extravagant riches?

Prayer is familiar, but it is hardly understood. The sad truth is that much of what we call prayer is man-centered, nothing more than selfish and desperate begging, proscribed ritual, or self-centered aggrandizement. "Thank You, God, for making *me* and *mine* greater, more favored, than the others (whoever they may be)." As a result, the consequences of prayer are not always what we want. We pray that our soldiers will be victorious, which means that the young men and women of those we call "enemy" will die.

Mark Twain wrote a powerful short story entitled *The War Prayer* on the unmentioned (but really wished for) consequences of prayer. Twain would not allow this book to be published until after his death, because he believed that the book was the truth and only dead men know the truth. In this book the protagonist, a strange old bearded man, comes into a church while the congregation is praying for victory for their young soldiers. Stating that he was sent by the Almighty, his mission was to tell the congregation just exactly what it was they were praying for. While praying for victory over the enemy, they were also praying for destruction of the enemy, the killing of their young men, leaving widows and fatherless children, for plague and pestilence to strike their lands, hunger and deprivation to strike the citizens of the enemy country, and all the evil things that happen in all wars. Of course, the congregation thought the old man was just crazy.

Prayer is an action, and all actions have consequences. The scientific community is now beginning to explore the positive affects of prayer in healing. There can be little doubt that prayers, at times, do have an effect. But the subtle actions of prayer are most often countermanded by other more powerful, more persistent actions. We pray for health, but our daily habits are far more powerful and persistent. We pray for peace, but hate and condemn our enemies. The constant fear and hatred in our hearts far outweigh the few pleading and sincere words for peace. Often the prayers we pray are nothing more than wishful thinking.

Prayer and the Warrior Sage

The warrior sage has a different perspective of prayer. She understands that prayer is a discipline, not an exercise in wishful thinking or empty praising. As a discipline, prayer demands both understanding and practice. It is not about how often or how long you pray, nor is it about the words you use. To experience the full power of prayer requires far more effort than simply repeating some rhyming couplet at meals or attending prayers at church, the synagogue, or the mosque. The word "discipline" indicates that there are crucial elements – surrender, focus, and awareness – that must be developed and refined in order to achieve a level of mastery. The intent of the discipline of prayer is to minimize, and eventually eliminate, the influence of the ego-self. It is about creating the mind-space necessary to experience the power of divine grace.

As we become more skilled within the discipline of prayer, we progress through three levels of prayer. These levels really represent an increasing ability to surrender ego-centered thought and action to the spiritual-Self and divine grace. As our skill develops, these levels evolve one into the other, bringing greater clarity and conscious experience of divine grace.

Briefly, the first stage of prayer involves learning to communicate to the divine. Most people do not engage prayer as a discipline, and consequently, do not move beyond this basic level of prayer. The second stage occurs when we begin to listen to God as much as we speak to God. Prayer then becomes a two-way communication between the individual and the divine. Most of us hardly know how to listen to one another let alone listen to the subtle, quiet voice of the divine. The third stage, achieved by only a few, begins the perfection of prayer. At this stage, one's entire life becomes a prayer, and speaking and listening become so ingrained that our actions are done in harmony with the divine. As we shall see later, the perfection of prayer demands great effort, and consequently, represents a rare achievement. Those who do achieve perfection make no claims, do not impose beliefs, and behave far differently than the rabble who often loudly and falsely claim they act in God's name. Understanding these three stages is easier if we explore the crucial elements that make up the discipline of prayer.

Surrender: The Offering of Self

In spiritual traditions, prayer is understood as an act of surrender, not a request or demand for outcome. Genuine prayer is God-centered as opposed to man-centered. In other words, not "my will be done" but "Thy will be done." Instead of begging for favors, it is recognition of the grace that is already present. Instead of a proscribed ritual, it is the honest communication of what is in one's heart. Simply put, prayer is an offering of oneself, and all that is of value to oneself.

The key element here is the term "surrender," often a stumbling block to those controlled by the ego-self. Many of us react both strongly and negatively to the term surrender. We all know of people who surrendered to some powerful ego, or to a movement, giving up any sense of responsibility for thinking their own thoughts. Cults flourish because there are many who willingly surrender their power of discrimination, and want to be told what to do, where to go, and what to believe. Many religions are really nothing more than cults, demanding slavish adherence to whatever dogmas the leader or head of the church decides. Politicians build political bases on strong party affiliations where individuals surrender their critical faculties and vote the party line. When this kind of surrender becomes extreme, we find fanaticism, religious fundamentalism, and ultimately, schizophrenia, where the individual hears fantasy voices that seem real, urging him to take some kind of drastic action.

This type of surrender, a negation of independent thought and action, is a denial of personal responsibility and power. It is a source of powerlessness and self-hatred. When we surrender independent thought and decision-making to another, to a belief system or to a government, we become victims, and stunt personal and spiritual growth. One of the most common manifestations of this kind of surrender is the fear of what others may think, arguably the greatest and most common fear in American culture. So we slavishly follow whatever trend the talking heads on TV and radio are promoting, and take great pains to fit in, to not criticize the president, especially in times of conflict and war. For so many, being "united" means following the standard line of whatever authority – religious, political or social – holds power their mind.

But this is *not* the surrender of prayer. What is demanded in prayer is surrender to the higher spiritual-Self. It is to experience the love that is the spiritual-Self, and to experience our inner strength. In this act, the little "I" of the ego-self loses its star-status, and takes its rightful place as a servant. Genuine surrender requires listening, trust, and acceptance. These are all actions that the ego-self, with its habitual need to control, strongly resists. That need to control is created by the emotional dependencies suffered by the ego-self. The more we cleanse our heart of emotional disturbances, the more effective our prayer becomes. This is the practical training for prayer that few of us ever receive.

Non-Attachment and Emotional Harmony

The practical way to achieve genuine surrender is to practice non-attachment. Non-attachment doesn't mean non-involvement. It means that we think, speak, and act free of dependencies that muddle our thinking and prevent us from understanding the reality around us. Non-attachment means that we don't "need," or psychologically own, a particular thing, person, or event in order to be content and secure. It stems from recognizing that things, events, and people do not make us secure or happy, and realizing that the source of our joy and security lies within the spiritual-Self. In this way, we are free to use and relate to all things of the world, and free from the burden of ownership.

To make prayer powerful, we must free ourselves from the negative emotions that interfere with prayer by creating stress, disharmony, and competing voices in our heart. To understand why non-attachment is so important, we need to briefly look at how we create negative emotions.* In yoga science, there is a clear distinction between negative emotions that lead to imbalance, stress, and suffering, and positive emotions, which lead to freedom, balance and harmony. These two categories of emotion have different sources. Negative emotions are a distortion of powerful and primitive drives which are natural elements of the physical body. Yoga science points out four instinctual urges, or primitive drives, inherent in our biological structure: self-preservation,

* For more detailed information, see *Strong and Fearless: The Quest for Personal Power.* Phil Nuernberger, Yes International Publishers, 2003.

hunger, sleep, and sex. These drives motivate us to protect ourselves from danger, seek out food for nourishment, give ourselves adequate rest for revitalization, and participate in the creation of new life so that the species will continue.

When one of these primitive urges is stimulated, such as self-preservation when we face danger (or think we do), it generates energy. This energy is quickly directed to a specific action, goal, or object that in the past has satisfied the underlying urge or drive. When this energy is given a specific direction or goal, it is called "desire," and becomes a compelling motivating force. All behavior is motivated by a desire of one kind or the other. We may have lots of wants and wishes, but we won't be moved to action until there is a desire, enough energy to move us toward achieving some goal.

If the object of our desire satisfies us in any way, the connection between the urge and the particular object is reinforced, and the desire for that particular object becomes stronger. Think of your favorite food. Every time you satisfy that desire by eating that particular food, you build the strength of the connection until it becomes a powerful habit in the mind. On the other hand, if we choose something that leads to pain or discomfort, we quickly learn to avoid that particular choice. Think about the time when you went to a restaurant and ate some food that was spoiled, and you became ill with nausea and vomiting. You probably never went back to that restaurant. Then that avoidance becomes a habit in the mind.

The more often we successfully use the object, person, or situation to satisfy a desire or avoid pain, the stronger the connection becomes. This connection between the desire and the object becomes so strong that the desire and the object come to be seen as one. At this point, we are dependent on that particular object, convinced that only that object (person, event, belief) will make us happy or secure. We forget that the source of our joy, our contentment, and our sense of security, lies within us, and is not caused by the object of our desires.

In this way, the habits of the mind, some helpful, some not, are created. The more powerful and disturbing habits are the fears and worries, the negative thinking, the guilt and self-hatred that create enormous stress, unhappiness, and disease. But just as unhelpful are the habits that say we must have this and that object in order to be accepted, happy, and fulfilled. All these desires, fears, and disappointments create a constant noise in the mind and heart, and interfere with prayer.

For example, there are many prayers for peace, but often those who pray are fearful, worried about possible terrorist attacks, or that they or their loved ones may be harmed. So these prayers originate in fear, are colored by fear and motives for revenge for past attacks, and concerned about material losses. Even though the words are peaceful, the subtle intent is far from peaceful, and while we pray for peace, a great part of the mind is engaged with fears of war and destruction. It's no wonder why so few of us actually experience the real power of prayer. Praying for peace is one thing, actually being peaceful in the heart is quite another.

The warrior sage understands that it is not the primitive drive or even desire that creates negative emotional states, but our dependency on the object of the desire. What makes us disturbed is our "need to have" a specific object, person, or event in order to be happy, safe, or whatever. There is always a threat that someone or something will prevent us from gaining, enjoying, or keeping the object of our desire. Even when we gain the desired object, it only strengthens our dependency on the object, and leads to even greater threats and danger. In other words, the more we invest in dependency, the greater the probability of negative emotions.

In our natural state, independent of any relationship, we have no emotional disturbance. When we quiet our thoughts, and focus attention to the center of the mind, we find that there is no fear, worry, or negative thoughts of any kind. At the core or center of every human mind, we experience only tranquility, or peace. Emotional disturbances exist only at the superficial levels of the mind, the level of sensory organization and habit.

Emotional disturbance always involves a dependency relationship to an object in the external world. Not a single negative emotion has an exclusively internal source; it always arises from a dependency attachment to a desired object, situation, or person. We can become emotionally disturbed whenever any desire is unfulfilled, blocked, or somehow threatened. This emotional disturbance creates patterns in the mind that distort perceptions and thinking, inhibit the creative force, and force us into more rigid forms of behavior that lead to imbalance and stress.

When we anticipate harm of any kind, through loss, a change of events, or the inability to gain what we need, the inevitable outcome is fear. And when we don't measure up to expectations and standards, we turn on ourselves and create self-hatred. Each and every emotional disturbance is based on some attachment, a condition of dependency. All of them are powerful habits in the mind, and each of these habits becomes a competing voice for prayer, interfering with the effectiveness of prayer.

The Discipline of Prayer

We cannot live without satisfying our needs and desires, nor would anyone want to stop having pleasure. Obviously, we are not going to stop eating, sleeping, having sex, or protecting ourselves. Nor should we become passive and accept whatever happens to come our way. The warrior sage is fully and actively engaged in the world, but does so from the perspective of non-ownership.

To accomplish this, he develops the discipline of prayer through the practice of surrender and non-attachment. As we can see, the discipline of prayer involves far more than the simple act of praying. It demands an active effort to bring balance into one's life through balancing and energy techniques, control and direction of emotional energies, and the practice of non-attachment.

The goal is to create a life of balance where stress is no longer a factor, and emotional disturbances are a thing of the past. As we become increasingly free of stress and its consequences, we are able to focus more effectively, think more clearly, and bring a greater focus and intensity to prayer. Through practice, the warrior sage takes control of emotional energy, directing it in positive ways rather than using it to create disturbances. In this way, prayer is done in a state of balance and harmony.

As we gain greater balance, we are able to refine and enhance our focusing and concentration skills. The more attention we bring to prayer, the more effective prayer becomes. As we discussed earlier, a distracted mind is a weak mind, and prayer done with a distracted mind has very little success. It is attention that makes the mind powerful. Prayer done with focused, undivided attention (free from emotional distractions) becomes a very different experience than prayer done with underlying distractions from competing desires, fears, and wants.

As we refine our concentration skills, particularly through meditation, we are able to create deeper and more profound states of silence and stillness. This, of course, leads to even greater awareness of the spiritual-Self, and prayer takes on more profound meaning and experience. As we gain greater skill in surrender and non-attachment, the consequence is greater balance, clarity, attention, and awareness. This allows us to gradually break through the barrier of the ego-self, and experience the spiritual-Self as grace. This is an opening to mystical knowledge, and the beginning of wisdom as a conscious skill.

Through surrender we experience humility, one of the most powerful resources of the spiritual-Self, and a defining quality of the sage. Prayer is a tool that leads to honest humility, the recognition that the individual ego-self is a small but integral part of something much greater. This is the secret power of prayer – the experience of love and the on-set of humility.

Humility – The Secret Power

Why do we call humility a secret? Because the modern American mind typically rejects humility. After all, winning is everything, so we must strive to be number one. We are taught as children to compete in nearly every aspect of life – beauty contests, little league, entry into private schools. We struggle to gain every possible advantage for ourselves and our children. This intense competitiveness, the rat race, plays out on a personal level, in the family, in the schools, in the culture, in the nation. Since only a few make it to the top, the rest are left to identify with a group of winners – a sports team, the corporation, the military, the biggest weapons, the most money, the most fame. Tying their identity to a winner, they can forget, for at least a little while, that they feel like they are the "losers" in life. We measure success in material terms: position, fame, power, money. Try speaking to a fast-moving executive about humility and you quickly learn that humility is not an American ideal by any stretch of the imagination.

For most, humility signifies some kind of deference or submission. In fact, this is the first definition of humility in *Webster's New Collegiate Dictionary*. But what humility means to the warrior sage is something quite different. For him, humility is the recognition that he is a small but integral part of something much greater than himself. Genuine humility arises from the mystical experience of wholeness or completeness, of experiencing one's own divine origins, and recognizing that divinity in everything you see. It is the experience of perfection that eliminates false pride; in fact, it eliminates the need for any pride at all.

Genuine humility is what we experience when we watch a child being born, or when we lie on our back gazing up at a clear and starry night, marveling at the unfolding heavens. It fills the heart with wonder, respect, and gratitude without diminishing us in any way. During these times, we never experience solitude as loneliness, nor do we feel isolated. At this time, we are free from the powerful grip of the ego-self, and all the petty needs and wants that this entails. We are small and great at the same time; there is no need to be better than, or any sense of being less than.

This wonder-filled freedom from the demands of the ego-self has enormous benefits. The warrior sage understands that prayer, as a rich source of humility, is a powerful tool for refining the ego-self, and breaking the strong and terrible bonds of egotism. For him, humility provides a powerful antidote to the egotistical arrogance that comes so easily with the acquisition of power. The only legitimate purpose for power of any kind is service to humanity. Yet, for the most part, as people become powerful, as nations become powerful, they become arrogant, using their economic, political, and military power to create empire and impose their will on others. Everyday humanity suffers from the arrogance of leaders who use power for their own benefit and aggrandizement.

For the warrior sage, there is no need for self-aggrandizement.

Being "number one!" has no appeal for the individual who realizes that he is a part of the divine. In Taoist philosophy, this humility is spoken of as "the way of water." Water always flows to the lowest point, yet nothing can resist water. Water never opposes, but flows around any obstacle, until the obstacle is washed away. Eventually, the largest stone is changed and moved by water. Humility never opposes, but in the end, moves all to its course.

The practice of any discipline leads to skill. As the warrior sage practices the discipline of prayer and becomes more and more skilled, he moves through the three stages of prayer. The process is continuous, and the stages are not discreet. As he gains in skill, each stage evolves and is continued in the next. But in each stage, he gains greater knowledge, power and wisdom until prayer itself is perfected.

First Stage: Talking to the Divine

Prayer is a communication of one's genuine feelings and thoughts to the divine. It is the most simple, honest and straightforward communication possible. There is no mediator, there is no facilitator, and there is no teacher, priest, or guru. There is no lying possible, for in prayer, only what is truly in your heart is the message, not necessarily the words that are spoken. Great and magnificent concepts, formal and elevated language, and learned and complex philosophies mean nothing at all. What impacts the mind, what influences the environment, and what reaches through the spiritual-Self to the greater divinity is what is true and experienced in the heart. We may speak wonderful words and phrases, but the secret fears, hatreds, and angers lying in the heart shout out far more powerfully.

All religious traditions are filled with stories and parables about how the naïve prayers of innocent children and uneducated people whose actions and/or words arise from the heart's truth achieve divine grace, whereas the prayers of the learned and anointed do little. One example is a story from the Russian Orthodox Church.

> A new leader (called the Metropolitan) had just been chosen to lead the church. He was a genuine person, very learned in the ways and traditions of the church. Being conscientious, he had a great desire to

serve the priests and monks under his charge. He traveled far and wide, visiting the different churches and monasteries and offering whatever assistance was needed. He came to know of a small monastery located on a tiny island on Lake Baikal. To his dismay, the records revealed that no Metropolitan had visited this small monastery for nearly thirty years. Apparently, there were only three monks there, and, according to church records, they had been left alone for all this time.

Wishing to correct this oversight, the Metropolitan immediately hired a large boat and set sail for the island. The three monks, now rather elderly, were overjoyed to be visited by their spiritual leader and made every effort to make him comfortable. The Metropolitan, concerned about their spiritual growth, asked the monks about their prayers.

"We have never been taught the formal prayers," said one of the monks. "So we simply pray, 'Thou are three and we are three. Bless us, O Lord'."

Smiling to himself at their naïveté, the Metropolitan kindly said, "Oh my, I can see that no one has taught you to pray the official prayers of the Church. Come, my friends, and I will teach you how to say the prayers."

The monks were overjoyed by this kindness and generosity. For several hours they listened to the official prayers taught by the Metro-politan. Finally, it was time for him to return to the far-off mainland.

The monks were grateful to the Metropolitan for giving so gener-ously of his time and knowledge. "Thank you, Holy Father," they said. "Your kind attention and instruction will be reverently received and practiced. Please pray for us that we may follow the correct path."

The Metropolitan gave his final blessings and sailed off. The religious leader was pleased with himself that he had taken the time and trouble to visit these poor, elderly monks and to teach them the proper way to pray.

Several hours into his journey, the skies darkened, and a great storm came upon the ship. The waves grew in size, and the ship was tossed here and there. Suddenly, as the Metropolitan watched the storm clouds, he was stunned by an amazing sight. Illuminated by great light-ning flashes, the three elderly monks were running as fast as they could above the surface of the waves toward the ship.

"Holy Father," they cried, as they came closer to the ship. "Please forgive us; we have forgotten the prayers you have so generously taught us. We want so much to pray to God in the right way. Please, be kind enough to repeat them for us once more."

The Metropolitan sank to his knees. "Forgive me," he said to the monks. "Please forget all that I so arrogantly taught you. Pray as you have always done, and be kind enough to pray for me that I might learn to pray as you three do."

Prayer is a focusing of attention, and whatever we pay attention to, we reinforce and strengthen in the mind. But what degree of attention do we have when we pray? In a moment, the thought is replaced with a competing thought, and the feeling is replaced with other feelings. The sad truth is that most prayers are nothing more than empty ritual, and all too often the individuals praying are more interested in the sound of their voice, or creating an impact on the gullible listener than experiencing the depth of feeling and surrender necessary for prayer to be effective.

The power of prayer stems from the ability to focus emotional energy. Prayer is an act of commitment, a channeling of emotional energy into purpose. But that purpose must necessarily be free of the wants, fears, and desires of the ego-self. When emotional energy is unconflicted, in harmony with the heart's truth, then prayer becomes a powerful and useful tool. Through God-centered prayer, the purity of the emotional energy opens the gate to spiritual power, an expression of divine will. Through prayer, we open ourselves to the experience of selfless love as we surrender to the overwhelming power of the divinity that lies within us. This experience is often referred to as "divine grace." However, if that emotional energy is directed by the ego-self for its own ends, then prayer is man-centered, and becomes nothing more than another shopping list for the ego-self, competing with all the other shopping lists of the ego-self.

Second Stage: Listening to the Divine

As the warrior sage gains greater balance and self-control, and becomes more skilled in surrender and non-attachment, she begins to listen more and speak less. In the second stage, communication becomes a two-way street as we learn to listen to the divine even more than we speak to the divine. We don't listen to hear the voice of God speaking from beyond the clouds, but instead, we listen to the "still, small voice" that arises from silence in our heart center.

Many claim to listen to God when all they really hear is the roaring voice of their own ego-self with its attendant needs for power, attention, fame, and fortune and its fears and desires. In the second stage, it is crucial that one remain alert to the subtle influences of the ego-self so that one really hears the divine and not the siren voices of the ego-self. To achieve this degree of skill with prayer demands absolute truthfulness with oneself, as well as accurate knowledge of one's own inner dragons.

Self-knowledge is the unique demand of the second stage. Unless we have insight into the structure of the mind, we can never be certain that the voice we hear is the voice of wisdom and not the fears and desires of the ego-self. There is no question that we have enormous capacity to fool ourselves, but we also have the capacity to honestly face ourselves. To accomplish this, we must become objective about the mind. That means that we must accept what the mind does without judging the mind as good or bad. Making judgments about good and bad immediately brings on the defense mechanisms of the mind, and we learn very little about its hidden structures.

Genuine self-acceptance means that we accept weaknesses with the same equanimity as we do strengths. This allows us to practice discrimination, the ability to discern cause/effect relationships. Through discrimination, we literally witness how the mind creates meaning and the consequences both useful and not useful. By witnessing the mind, we become aware of how we create disturbances for ourselves and others. We can't rely on analyzing the mind because what we use to analyze the mind is the mind itself. The mind provides us with plenty of answers, some may even be accurate, but we have no power to do things differently.

Instead, the warrior sage practices discrimination, the discernment of cause/effect relationships. By not judging the mind, we are able to clearly witness the thoughts and patterns of the mind, and the consequences of our thoughts. This self-awareness allows greater choice as to which patterns (useful ones) we pay attention to and which patterns (destructive ones) we simply witness and let fall by the wayside. In this way we gradually train the mind and ego-self to run helpful patterns and habits and to not give energy or expression to unhelpful patterns and habits.

This process demands genuine humility. If we have a need to be important, to be "in control," and its "our way or the highway," we cannot be honest with ourselves, and consequently, we won't be honest with others. The strength of a warrior sage is her indifference to these ego-needs. This dramatically impacts how she treats others, and their response to her. Without a growing humility, self-knowledge is extremely difficult, if not impossible.

As we learn to listen to that "still, small voice" we are actually learning to listen to our true conscience. Most people think that their conscience is that part of their mind that tells them that they are good or bad. But this judging is nothing more than the habits we learn from our parents, teachers, preachers, peers, and other policemen of behavior.

Our real conscience is the pure intellect of the mind, that power of discrimination that discerns cause/effect relationships. The true conscience never judges good or bad, it simply points out consequences that we will find helpful or unhelpful.

When we use this power of discrimination, this pure intellect, to understand the world, we gain insight, vision, and intuitive knowledge. When we use this power in self-reflection, we know what course of action is most useful for us, and which course of action will result in pain and unhappiness.

When we turn this power towards the spiritual-Self, we gain wisdom and the mystical experience. It is the practice of inner concentration, silence, and stillness that leads to spiritual knowledge. At this point, we listen to the divine with confidence and accuracy, by-passing the wants, needs, and fears of the little ego-self completely. As we grow in self-knowledge and refine the capacity to listen, we gain skill in listening to the divine.

This growing capacity leads to the third stage, the perfection of prayer. The warrior sage understands that prayer is far more than speaking and listening to God, it is the source of a great power – the ability to live in harmony and strength, free from the ravages of stress and emotional disturbance. This is the natural outcome when the discipline of prayer is perfected.

The Perfection of Prayer

It isn't what we say that makes prayer perfect, it is how we live. The inner discipline of prayer becomes perfect when one's entire life becomes prayer. Through commitment and practice, every thought, word and deed becomes an act of surrender to the divine. In other words, the warrior sage creates a life of selfless service. This requires an enormous commitment, but the payoff is even greater. This has nothing to do with being nice, or being "holy." It is an exercise in true personal power, creating a life of deep harmony, free from all stress and emotional disturbance. We achieve this deep harmony only by gaining access to the mystical experience of grace, and the eventual perfection of an attitude of non-attachment. Everything belongs to the divine. The warrior sage is free to use everything, and everything is there for him to use, but he owns nothing. He recognizes that the spiritual-Self alone, the on-board representative of the divine, is the source of all security, joy, and contentment.

It is in the perfection of prayer that the tantric spiritual principle of action (discussed in Chapter 3) is fulfilled on the human plane. At this point, the warrior sage acts in spontaneous harmony. There really is no freedom of choice, because there is no alternative to harmony. This does not mean that his actions are determined. Far from it. There is no determination because habit no longer rules the choice. What rules behavior is harmony. In this way, the warrior sage always seems to know exactly the right move, even if that move is seen by others to be arbitrary, capricious, or even wrong. In the light of hindsight, these actions will always be understood as timely, effective, and "correct."

The same principle is found in Taoist philosophy, where it is said that the sage does nothing, by which all things are accomplished. This does not mean that Taoism is a "do nothing" philosophy as one noted professor of Chinese History so mistakenly stated. It means that actions are spirit-centered rather than ego-centered, and thus are accomplished through deep harmony. They become effortless. So the personality, the mind/body complex regulated, but not controlled, by the ego-self, really does nothing. In this perfection of prayer and the achievement of deep harmony, all actions are effortless.

This is not strange, since we all do this at times. Simply recall a time when you were so focused on what you are doing that you forgot about time. During this event, you are not worried about anything, you aren't beating up on yourself, or spending time in negativity, you are simply doing what is there to do with your best efforts and results. In fact, this experience is so powerful that we often refer to this as a peak experience. Our actions are in harmony with the demands of the situation, and we do our very best at that moment.

The perfection of prayer leads to integrity where word, thought, and deed are in harmony and consistent with each other. And the great conflict that most of us experience, of doing what we don't want to do or what we know we shouldn't do, or knowing what to do and not being able to do it, is forever eliminated. By making his life a prayer, the warrior sage achieves total integrity between his inner being and his outer expression. His integrity inspires and influences others, allowing him to lead without compelling and to direct others for their benefit rather than his own.

Discipline, Levels, and the Experience of Grace

The transformative power of prayer lies in the mystical experience, also called grace. Grace is an inner experience unrelated to any external event or outcome that was prayed for. For most, success at prayer is linked to having a favorable outcome, and they "thank God" for answering their prayers. It's interesting to note that few, if any, thank God for not getting the favorable outcome they petitioned for. This childish view of divinity and prayer often produces a false faith that eventually ends in arrogance or fatalism. At best, it is misleading, and prevents the individual from experiencing grace, the greatest benefit of prayer. At worst, it creates unhealthy dependency and feelings of powerlessness.

The warrior sage recognizes that any achievement takes knowledge and effort, awareness and skill. For her, the discipline of prayer is not a task, but an opportunity to walk in the presence of the divine, to experience grace as a living reality, a presence that is the very essence of life.

We experience grace in a number of different ways, depending on the level of prayer that we master, and the intensity of our effort. In the first level, we often experience it as an inner strength that comes when we have exhausted every means that we have. At this time, grace allows us to continue our good efforts and often is the leverage upon which success is obtained.

We may experience grace as a transcendent tranquility, a sense of peace that is so profound that it surpasses all understanding. In times of loss it is the vehicle that takes us past any grief, and lets us know that even in the darkest of times, the light is always present. We may experience grace as an acceptance, an experience of great harmony even though strife is all around. Each individual experiences it in their own way, but for each, the grace resolves all doubts, fears, worries and concerns.

As we expand our capacity, our experience becomes more intense and complete, removing lingering doubts and fears. This is particularly true when we evolve into the second level of prayer. As we begin to hear the subtle, quiet voice of the divine within ourselves, we begin to understand the pathway before us. We begin to experience grace as divine guidance, a source of great wisdom that speaks to us out of the great stillness and silence. Along with this wisdom comes a growing sense of inner tranquility and peace. There is a refuge within that no one can disturb, and that is accessible and available to us at any time.

As we grow in experience and skill, and our life becomes a living prayer, we experience the presence of the divine in all that we do. This experience is one of an unshakable joy that pervades everything we do. We still experience the pleasure and pain, success and failure, gain and loss, that is part and parcel of life, but we never lose awareness of the fundamental joy of our creator. At this point, our lives are no longer our own as we move in harmony with the Spirit, accepting the vagaries of life with equanimity.

For the warrior sage, the discipline of prayer is life-long. There is no final destination, no final goal to complete. The practices, tools, and knowledge of the discipline constitute an ongoing process. It is an important part of the journey for each of us, but it is only part of the journey. For prayer to be successful, the other spiritual disciplines of meditation and contemplation are also necessary. And while the benefits of prayer are significant, the warrior sage recognizes that they are only part of the spiritual journey. We turn now to the second spiritual discipline, that of meditation, the path of the mind.

Chapter Six
Meditation–Pathway of the Mind

*Meditation helps in transcending national, religious, and traditional boundaries
and expands individual consciousness into cosmic consciousness.*
—His Holiness Swami Rama—

The spiritual discipline of prayer provides a foundation for meditation through the experience of grace and the development of humility. Grace is understood simultaneously as the consequence of sincere, committed effort and devotion on the part of the individual as well as a gift given by the divine. In prayer, divinity is first experienced as an external power, particularly in the early stages. Through surrender, the individual is accepted and embraced by the divinity. As realization dawns of the inner reality of the spiritual-Self, prayer becomes affirmation of the grace that is already present.

Rather than surrender and humility, the goal of meditation is personal power on all levels – spiritual, mental, and material. Meditation is the path of the mind, refining concentration and inner awareness to gain greater access to the powerful resources of the mind, and develop them as conscious skills. As we become more skilled in meditation, awareness expands to the underlying spiritual-Self and its unlimited resources. Personal power is the hallmark of the warrior sage, and the discipline of meditation is how that power is systematically developed.

First and foremost is spiritual power, the direct experience of divinity as our true identity. This direct, conscious experience of the spiritual-Self (*samadhi* in yogic terminology, the "mystical experience" in western terminology) is the single most important goal of the discipline of meditation. Spiritual power arises naturally as we consciously access the spiritual-Self and enter the portal to Universal Consciousness and infinite power. As we access the spiritual-Self, we simultaneously gain access to all the resources of the mind. For the warrior sage, both spiritual power and mind power are required to live and work effectively in the world. Through direct experience and insight, she recognizes that the ultimate source of all power lies within the spiritual dimension.

Radiant Matter: Mind as Instrument

Meditation is the pathway of the mind, but what is meant by the term mind? The great spiritual traditions of self-mastery and Self realization recognize the human mind as the instrument of knowledge. Different spiritual disciplines vary in their descriptive psychologies and philosophies, but essentially all agree that the mind is the tool through which knowledge is revealed. In yoga science, the mind is called the *antahkarana*, or "inner instrument". The mind is not the brain, but a cohesive field of energy held in unity by the ego function. This field of energy is often described as radiant matter in yoga science.

From the perspective of yoga science, the mind consists predominantly of *satvas* energy. The quality or nature of *satvas* energy is to reveal, to illuminate, or to unveil. In its purest form, this *satvas* energy forms the function of discrimination, called *buddhi* in yoga science. This function is considered to be pure intellect, and through discrimination has the ability to reveal or discern difference and even the most subtle cause/effect relationships. The *buddhi*, or pure intellect, is involved in the process of creating the reality in which we live, and thus reveals/ understands reality as it actually is, not as we learn to see it. As the seat of the intellect, the *buddhi* is the foundation for analytic reasoning and decision-making in the human mind. We will further explore the power of this intellect in the next chapter.

From this power to know, to reveal, arises the ego-function that, in its boundary function, creates the limited ego-self. Out of the ego function emerges the sensory mind and the sense capacities. The function of the sensory mind is to interact through the physical senses of the body with the external reality to create a personal reality.

To repeat, it is the essential nature and function of mind to know, to reveal. We each create the reality that we live by the way our individual mind creates meaning. But this meaning is created out of what already is given. In this way, we speak of mind as revealing. What is revealed is already there, but the revelation process is a creative process as we engage in creating the interpretation that becomes our personal reality. For example, gravity has eternally existed, but until Newton "revealed" some of its laws or regularities, it was not understood. Newton didn't create gravity, he became aware (revelation) of gravity in a way that allowed him to formulate an understanding of it. Another way of saying this is that the mind is akin to a filter mechanism by which we filter out only a very small part of the whole, and this very small part becomes our personal reality.

Once Newton communicated his insight, others could bring attention to the field and expand awareness of this aspect of reality. Newton's perspective of gravity was a scientific breakthrough, but certainly far from complete. As other minds entered the same field as Newton, gradually the limitations of Newton's understanding began to give way to further insights and development. The modern quantum physicist is not creating knowledge, but rather finding new and more subtle ways to understand the physical reality. The reality of gravity existed before Newton, is much more than what Newton understood, and still exists today. It is the revealing nature of intellect that allows us to understand gravity, quantum physics, and everything else, at more and more sophisticated levels or dimensions. Human beings do not create reality, they create ways of understanding what already exists; and that understanding becomes personal reality.

We utilize both the mind and the body in order to create understanding. The mind works by utilizing the neural fields created by the brain. The quality and the strength of the neural field determine the depth and penetration into the infinite knowledge fields that already exist in the universal whole, or God. Neural fields are defined by the qualities and limits of the particular brain engaged. If there is brain damage, the instrument is limited and access to knowledge states will be affected. But that doesn't give us indication of the quality of the individual mind. It only tells us about the quality of the hardware, the brain.

In a very real sense, each one of us creates our own unique personal reality, but one that is shared by those who create the same kind of meaning/reality. For example, a dog creates fields that are shared and understood by other dogs, all of which share in the same "doggy" field. Human beings create fields – mathematics, music, art, and so forth – which are participated in, shared by, all humans. Cultures are coherent fields created by closely-knit groups. To the extent we share the same fields, we understand each other.

Depending on his level of skill, the warrior sage develops the power to enter any and all fields. Through the natural capacity of mind to reveal (to create knowledge), anything can be understood, even the doggy field. We really don't know what the limits of the mind are. We do know that our skill in utilizing the mind is limited. The discipline of meditation is the unlearning of limits accomplished through attention and increasing awareness. As we refine attention to achieve concentration, and refine concentration to achieve meditation, we develop the strength and awareness necessary to enter into any knowledge field. This is genuine power, and it is the purpose of the discipline of meditation.

The mind, as an instrument of knowledge, already has the capacity. We don't need to learn how to understand; we need to understand how to learn. This involves several steps:
• Develop and refine the power of the mind through concentration;
• Expand awareness of the innate capacities of the mind through inner concentration;
• Become skilled in the use of these capacities through application and appropriate techniques;
• Refine inner awareness through meditation to directly experience the spiritual-Self and establish one's identity with the spiritual-Self. In this way, power flows out of the spiritual-Self, nullifying the limitations and problems inherent in the ego-self.

Through the discipline of meditation, the warrior sage removes ignorance, gains access to, and acquires skill in directing, the powerful resources of the mind. This power is inherently personal, and brings enormous capacity to the individual who develops it. This does not necessarily mean that this power will be used wisely or for the benefit of others. A powerful mind does not automatically become a spirit-centered mind.

Because concentration and meditation lead to enhanced capacity and power, the great sages are always careful to develop the humility of the individual as they guide the individual through the meditative disciplines into power. The humility gained through prayer and the wisdom and compassion gained through a growing spiritual awareness ensures that the power gained through meditation is used in service to others rather than for the needs and desires of the ego-self.

Attention, Attention, Attention

To understand the discipline of meditation,* we must first understand the critical necessity of attention and concentration in everything we do. It doesn't matter what you do – work as a laborer, student, stay-at-home mother with children, high-powered CEO, truck driver– the day we can't focus attention, nothing works for us. As discussed in Chapter 4, the most critical personal skill we have as an individual is the ability to focus attention. Learning, memory, performance, understanding, perception – everything we do begins with attention. Yet very few of us receive training in concentration techniques. Amazingly, the most critical personal skill that we have is left to haphazard development.

The warrior sage recognizes that human beings are far more than biological systems. At a far more profound and fundamental level, we are energy beings. No one can develop or even explain concentration by studying brain chemistry or brain waves. However, if we look at the mind as a subtle field of energy, concentration becomes relatively simple to grasp. More importantly, it becomes clear how to develop this crucial ability.

---

* For a more complete explanation, as well as techniques to build refined concentration and meditation skills, see *Strong and Fearless, The Quest for Personal Power.*

We can use the analogy of a light bulb to quickly grasp concentration. The smallest particle of light is called a photon. We are able to see because of photons bouncing off objects. (Remember, as was mentioned earlier, the eyes don't see objects, the eyes only register light waves, patterns of photons.) If you would hold out your hand in a room, you would easily "see" your hand, but you wouldn't feel the photons bouncing off your skin. By the time these photons arrive to bounce off and illuminate your hand, these photons are scattered and very weak after traveling a great distance and striking other sub-atomic particles. Consequently, we don't normally "feel the light". If someone does come into the room, hands raised on high, claiming to "Feel the Light" – better grab hold of your wallet!

However, if you put your hand right next to a light source, such as a lit 100-watt bulb, there would be a great number of them striking your hand with some force and you would feel the photons streaming off the light bulb as heat. Now, if we take these photons and synchronize them, force them to all go in the same direction at the same time, we build a very powerful light called a laser. And depending on how we build the laser, it could be powerful enough to burn through metal, or precise enough to do very delicate brain and eye surgery. In other words, when we synchronize the energy, it becomes powerful.

The same is true of the energy of the mind. Just for fun, let's call the individual units of energy of the mind "*mentons*." Typically, the mind's energy is scattered over a thousand different thoughts and directions. But when we synchronize these *mentons*, just as we synchronized the photons, then we create a powerful, focused mind, a laser-mind that can accomplish anything. The key is our ability to focus, to synchronize and coordinate the energy of the mind. This is concentration – synchronized, coordinated mind energy directed towards a specific point.

Concentration: Refined Attention

Once we understand the energy dynamics of the mind, concentration becomes easy to think about and the way is open to systematically expand our ability to concentrate. The more we synchronize mind energy, the stronger the neural field we create, the greater our concentration.

The conscious mind becomes focused fairly quickly and easily. As our focus becomes stronger, and we synchronize more and more mentons, our concentration deepens, and the capacity to understand increases. Another way of saying this is that the stronger (more synchronized) and more complete the neural field we create, the more focused, or concentrated, we become. The greater our concentration, the greater is our ability to penetrate knowledge fields, and the more complete our understanding.

Until we strengthen the synchronization, we can be easily distracted. The more often we are distracted, the greater the habit becomes of being distracted, and the less able we are to maintain a focus. In our fast-paced culture, with its constant bombardment of stimulus, we are doing a good job of training minds to be distracted. Modern culture is dominated by constantly changing stimuli. We are being conditioned by fast food, fast answers, and fast action. We are truly a nation of speed freaks. The consequences are evident in the increasing number of individuals with Attention Deficit Disorder, the growing impatience with everything that isn't immediately resolved, and the frantic pace of everyday life. Any experienced teacher, someone who has taught for twenty years, will tell you that it is increasingly impossible to get children to stay focused on task. Speak to any large audience for any length of time over twenty to thirty minutes, and you see those under the age of thirty-five or so have difficulty staying focused on the topic.

The problem is that genuine understanding, both in breadth and depth, takes time and focus. Very often, the fast answers that we find to difficult problems lead to even greater problems later on because we did not take the time to understand all the subtle aspects of the problems we faced. A clear example of this is when we enter a war that is supposed to be over in a matter of months, and find that we have entered a quagmire of death that lasts for years, and leads to hatreds and other problems that last for generations.

Training the mind to sustain focus, to be concentrated, is the most important learning that we can do. There are many ways to train concentration, but the most effective is to keep attention focused on a single point over time. This trains the mind to be still and quiet – not to jump from one thought to another, from one focus point to another. Training concentration demands a single focus point, such as a gaze on a fixed point. And not just any point. What we pay attention to leads to consequences. Focus points must be chosen carefully and purposefully in order to enhance the power of concentration as well as to bring balance to the mind/body system. For example, many people focus on what they fear. This creates all sorts of problems, from stress and disease, to a closing down of the mind. Ultimately, this continued focus creates conditions in the mind and consequently, in the behavior of the individual, that helps actualize whatever it is they fear.

Traditional schools of martial arts, such as karate, kung fu, taijiquan, and aikido, use the body and breathing to train concentration skills. One of the most sophisticated ways of using the body to train concentration is classical hatha yoga. The postures are designed to work with the body to expand awareness of both mind and body. Classical hatha yoga systematically proceeds from physical exercises to breathing exercises to mental exercises all to achieve a higher level of awareness through concentration.

The best way to train concentration is to use what is most natural to the mind, such as the breath and gazes. Since we depend so heavily on the sense of sight, it is a natural and convenient way to train the mind. In yoga science, this is called *trataka*, or gaze. When we hold a gaze, the eyes are not allowed to move off the target object or even blink, and the body is very still. We focus all of our attention on the object, and ignore all other thoughts and sensations, until the eyes begin to water, or concentration is involuntarily broken by blinking. At that point, we close the eyes and rest, or visualize the object internally. (One caveat: do not wear glasses or contacts when you practice a gaze.) By training the mind to stay focused and the eyes not to blink, we create a stronger, more cohesive, and synchronized energy. In other words, we become more concentrated.

Curiosity: The Driving Force

In general, we pay attention to anything for two fundamental reasons: interest or fear. The more interested we are in something, the more attention we pay. Of course, the more attention we pay, the more aware we are of whatever we direct our attention to. As Graph 6:1 illustrates, awareness expands as concentration increases. Interest and attention become mutually reinforcing, leading to an ever-expanding level of awareness. The more aware we become, the greater our capacity to understand whatever it is we are focused on. The essential key to effective learning/education is the level of interest one brings to the subject.

Graph 6:1

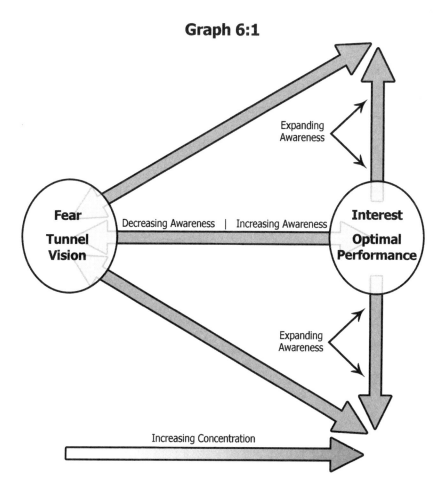

This is why curiosity is so critical to the human mind. The stronger our curiosity, the more we pay attention, and the greater our awareness becomes. Great scientists are tremendously curious people. They become so focused on what they are curious about that nothing else matters much to them. In all true spiritual traditions, the individual is encouraged to continually search for greater understanding. Curiosity is the motivation of the desire for knowledge. The great sages of the meditative traditions hold that the desire for higher knowledge is the one desire that should be nourished because that is the only desire that leads to freedom.

For a child, curiosity is natural. As neuro-science points out, the human brain is designed to learn. Curiosity and exploration are essential for proper neural development, and this continues throughout all of life. When we punish children for being curious, we damage that child's ability to learn and to grow as an individual on all levels. The warrior sage purposefully nurtures his curiosity, continuing to learn and explore throughout his entire life.

On the other hand, whatever we fear (or worry about) also grabs our attention. But fear has a dramatically different impact on the mind. As Figure 6:1 illustrates, fear will focus our attention, but it constricts our awareness. The greater our fear, the more fixated we become on the problem, and the harder it becomes to come up with creative solutions and alternatives. We suffer from "tunnel vision" and all we can see or think of is the problem itself. At this point, we can't even see the obvious.

Fear literally destroys genuine concentration. Instead of synchronizing the subtle energies of the mind, fear disrupts them, intensifying emotional cross-currents. At this point, genuine concentration becomes impossible, and we suffer from pseudo-concentration: the conscious mind is focused but the powerful unconscious mind is increasingly disorganized. In pseudo-concentration, the body becomes tense, thinking is clouded and grows more rigid, we behave in compulsive and awkward ways, and even our physical movements become awkward, jerky, and unbalanced.

The warrior sage understands that fear is a mind-killer, and every effort is made to become completely fearless. By eliminating fear and self-hatred, and being interested in what we are doing, we create a positive energy for ourselves. The greater our concentration, the more calm and sensitive we become, and the greater the power of the mind to penetrate and understand knowledge fields and the realities we face. The bridge between the resources of our inner world and the challenges and demands of the outer world is secure.

The Opening of Awareness

When we refine and enhance our natural capacity for attention, we develop the power of concentration. The greater our concentration, the more effective and powerful our mind becomes. We understand situations more clearly, we solve problems more effectively, and our memory becomes sharper. In short, the ability to concentrate determines how effective we are at just about anything we do. The key to this effectiveness is rarely recognized, but lies in the impact that concentration has on levels of awareness.

The most powerful physical, mental, and spiritual resources typically lie below normal awareness. This is true at all levels. For instance, we know that the body has an incredible capacity to heal itself. Biofeedback works by increasing the individual's awareness of the internal physical controls that already exist in the body. The principle that underlies biofeedback states that if you can become conscious of an on-going physiological event, such as blood flow, heart rate, endocrine response, or neural events, you can learn to direct and control that event.

We have unlimited capacity to regulate what happens in the body, even to the point of redirecting blood flow away from cancer in order to starve cancer cells. The reality is that we can't, and don't, use these controls because we are unaware of them. Consequently, we have no skill in using them. If you had the same awareness of your blood flow that you have of the fingers on your dominant hand, cancer would not be any threat to you at all. Like moving your fingers, you would simply alter your blood flow. Biofeedback works because it increases awareness of the controls and capacities that are already there!

The same is true for every mental resource that we have. Some individuals have what seems to be a natural capacity to envision the future. This powerful ability depends on the mind's capacity for discrimination, the ability to discern (to be aware of) the most subtle cause/effect relationships so clearly that we understand the future consequences. This power of discrimination is not subject to the limitations of time/space so necessary for sensory organization. Consequently, the mind has the power to be clearly aware of future events as well look dispassionately at past events.

This power of discrimination is not strange. We all occasionally have insights about what to do or not to do. These often come in the guise of a very quiet thought, such as "better not do that." But the desire, fear, or habit at the sensory level of the mind is loud and noisy, often overpowering that subtle, quiet thought. Later on, after we have already gone and done what we "better not do," and everything begins to fall apart, we tell ourselves, "I knew I shouldn't have done that!" And we did know; we just didn't pay attention. Only a few individuals become visionaries because only a few develop the awareness necessary to access that subtle level of intellect and use it as a conscious skill.

Spiritual knowledge is based solely on the direct experience that arises out of expanded awareness. Beliefs are useful in that they direct our attention, and through attention we expand awareness of the spiritual-Self. But belief is belief, not awareness. As was discussed earlier, most people mistakenly assume that if they believe something, they know it. Again, there is a difference between feeling hunger (awareness) and thinking that you are hungry. Direct experience, direct awareness, is absolutely necessary for spiritual knowledge.

Directing Focus

Another key dimension is whether the concentration has an external or an internal focus. Graph 6:2 illustrates the difference between external concentration and internal concentration, or meditation. It also illustrates the extreme difference between pseudo-concentration and true concentration. As the graph shows, intense fear always leads to drastic pathological outcomes. Most of us do not go to these extremes, but whatever fear we create for ourselves inhibits our ability to function effectively. As stated above, fear contracts awareness and limits the mind, precluding the inner awareness necessary to access the subtle powers of the mind. Most of us do not reach the extremes of psychosis or obsessive compulsive disorder, but we do spend a lot of time being neurotic, being distracted by petty fears and worries that devour our competency and happiness. Even a little fear begins to close down the mind and disturb the systems of the body. The greater the fear, the more difficult it is to access these resources. Even worse, fear prevents spiritual development. No one ever achieves spiritual awareness or enlightenment through fear! The warrior sage makes it a first priority to eliminate fear from the mind because of its negative impact.

The second point is the difference between internal concentration and external concentration. External focus, the most familiar to us, increases awareness of the external environment. Most of us have had what is often referred to as a "peak experience." Think back to a time when you were so focused and involved with what you were doing that time stood still. At that time you probably did your best work, you certainly weren't worrying or being hard on yourself, and you enjoyed every minute. We all have had peak experiences where time seems to stand still, actions are effortless, and we are at our most creative and productive. There are a number of writers who speak about "being in the flow" or "being in the zone" which are descriptive terms for peak experiences.

The warrior intentionally refines his powers of external concentration in order to access and develop the power of the mind and perform at optimal levels. As noted before, everything we do depends on our capacity to focus attention. Among the many benefits of refined concentration are:

1. Enhanced coordination between body and mind for greater balance and flexibility;

2. Greater perceptual sensitivity for enhanced communication skills, refined instincts, and greater clarity of thought;

3. Heightened ability to form accurate and penetrating knowledge for enhanced learning potential and intuitive knowledge.

In other words, the greater the skill at concentration, the more effective we become. But the real power of concentration becomes evident when we turn our focus inward, and expand our awareness of our powerful inner resources of the mind and body. It is inner concentration that develops the powerful qualities of the warrior and leads to the unique qualities of the sage. When we turn concentration to an inner focus, we develop the discipline of meditation.

Graph 6:2

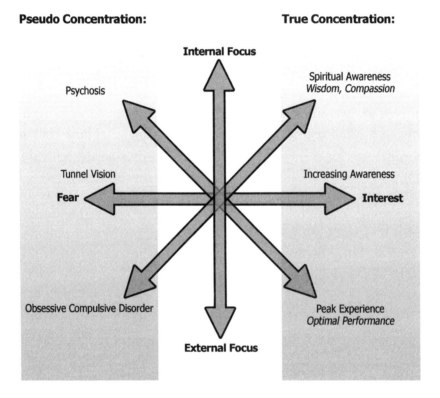

Pseudo Concentration:

True Concentration:

Internal Focus

Psychosis

Spiritual Awareness
Wisdom, Compassion

Tunnel Vision

Increasing Awareness

Fear

Interest

Obsessive Compulsive Disorder

Peak Experience
Optimal Performance

External Focus

Meditation: Refined Inner Concentration

Just as we refine attention to achieve concentration, we refine concentration to achieve meditation. Meditation is the most sophisticated method to train concentration skills. The term meditation is used in a variety of different ways, but in this context it has a specific meaning.

Meditation is not thinking about something, it is not a religious concept, it isn't even a philosophical concept. Meditation is a specific and highly technical scientific term indicating a specific state of attention. *Meditation is an unbroken stream of effortless concentration on a single internal point over an extended period of time.* The key elements of meditation are that it is unbroken, effortless, internal, single-pointed, and extended.

In other words, meditation occurs when inner concentration is refined to the point that concentration is effortless. This is quite different, and often far more difficult to achieve than external concentration. Concentration exercises focus on an external point, but meditation is an internal process, and more difficult to master. The focus points of meditation are only three – a thought, an image, or a sensation – because these constitute the entire content of the mind. The choice of which focus point to use – which thought, image, or sensation – depends on the skill of the individual and the purpose of the meditation. The meditative disciplines are very particular about the choice of focus points. They understand that whatever you focus on has impact on the mind beyond just training concentration.

For example, the use of mantras is a highly refined and sophisticated science based on the impact of sound on the energy patterns of the mind. In tantra yoga systems, mantra science is detailed, specific, and intentional. Just any thought, or any sound, is not acceptable. One western author, a physician who writes about meditation, recommends that people use the word "one" as a focus point for meditation. It is true that using the thought "one" will focus the mind, but what is the impact on the subtle levels? What knowledge field is associated with this inner sound of the thought "one"?

Mantra science is based on thousands of years of experimentation, research, and documentation. Mantras are chosen because of their documented impact on the energy field of the mind. This impact is created through the repetition of the thought itself, such as in "bija" or "seed" mantras which have no lexical meaning. Other mantras, which carry meaning, create impact through the intent of the meaning of the word. Within any tradition, mantras are carefully chosen for their specific impact, not simply used as a focus point for concentration.

The warrior sage carefully works within a meditative tradition in order to fully develop all aspects of meditation. Along with mantras, there are specific geometric symbols that represent the form of the sound of mantras. These symbols are referred to as yantras, and are often used in advanced states of meditation. Subtle vibrations are also meditation focus points, such as the energy centers called chakras. Like mantras, these focal points are carefully selected to deepen awareness of spiritual dimensions, but can also be used to create mental states that lead to specific material goals.

Perception – Not Thought

Key to understanding meditation as a process is to realize that thinking and perception are two different events in the mind. Meditation is not about thinking; it is a purely perceptual process. Meditation is actually refining the process of observation. You become a witness to the activities of the mind.

For example, when using a mantra, the intent is to hear the mind think the mantra, to listen to the sound of the mantra, not think about it. At first, learning how to listen to your mind instead of thinking with the mind seems a bit odd. But as you gain greater skill at listening (as you become more the observer rather than the thinker), you begin to discern subtle movements of sound. Eventually, you experience the vibration of the sound (mantra), which gradually leads to a profound silence in the mind. This silence is the opening to what is called *shunya*, or the void, an experience of nothingness, or "no-thingness." This is not an experience of emptiness, even though there is no content in the mind, no object of awareness, but rather, an experience of fullness, and absolute tranquility. Continuing in this state leads directly into the mystical experience, or awareness of the spiritual-Self.

Meditation is a process of refining your observational skills. If you *think* you are meditating, you are definitely not. Meditation and its ends are purely the outcome of observation (perception). If you have a question as to whether you have achieved this state, you haven't. The experience itself provides incontrovertible proof of the experience. You may try to convince yourself that you are enlightened, and maybe even fool others, but the truth is in the power of the experience. You cannot pretend and accomplish anything. Direct experience of the spiritual-Self is not susceptible to clever philosophizing, nor can it be faked.

As you refine concentration on an inner focus point, your awareness of the subtleties of mind increase. This is the consequence of meditation, not an intentional process of meditation. Meditation is not a technique for exploring the non-conscious elements of the total mind, it is a process to pierce the veil of mind into the super-conscious state (*samadhi*, or the mystical experience). As the warrior becomes more and more skilled in *samadhi*, the entire mind becomes an object of consciousness. It is not the mind observing itself as many in psychiatry and psychology like to think, but rather moving one's identity into the spiritual-Self (pure Consciousness) and allowing mind to be the object of consciousness.

The warrior understands that the mind is not conscious in and of itself; it is actually an object of consciousness. Mind seems conscious not because of neural activity, but because consciousness pervades the mind. Recall from our earlier discussion that pure Consciousness is the spiritual-Self. As we gradually experience this spiritual-Self as our true identity, the mind becomes more and more an object for us to study and understand. It is through this increasing inner awareness that we develop the power and qualities that define the warrior sage.

The Power of Inner Awareness

There are compelling reasons to become skilled in meditation. Recall that the more focused we become, the greater our expansion of awareness. This expanded awareness is the crucial element underlying the many benefits of meditation. Graph 6:3 illustrates the inner resources that become available for skill development due to the increased awareness generated by meditation.

The mind and body hold powerful resources that provide us with everything we need to be successful. Because we remain unaware of these resources, we do not develop them as conscious skills. For example, there are times when we instinctively know that something has happened to our child or someone close to us, yet we don't have the ability to use this powerful capacity for instinct as a conscious tool. It only seems to happen occasionally, and there seems no way to utilize this powerful resource whenever we want. There are times when we are able to think very clearly, or have a great insight about some problem or issue that bothers us. But like instinct, these times seem to happen to, or for us, and its not something that we consciously choose or can control.

Graph 6:3 lists the major inner resources available to the expanded awareness of the warrior sage in order of, and for, increasing depth and subtlety. For example, as we gain greater self-awareness, we become sensitive to when we are stressed out, and more quickly take steps to rebalance the system. When we become aware of our breathing, for instance, we can shift the unconscious habit of chest breathing and re-establish even, diaphragmatic breathing, and rebalance the autonomic nervous system, eliminating stress completely.

Graph 6:3

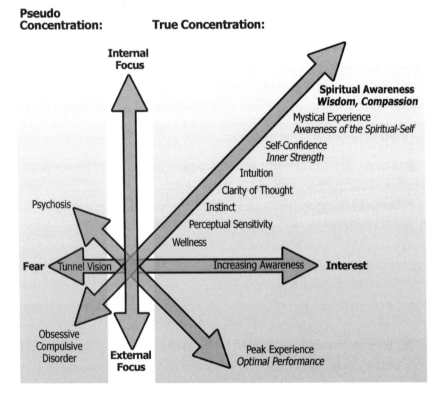

Through meditation, we gain access to all three knowledge states of the mind: analytic knowledge, instinct and intuition. Consequently, the warrior sage develops a penetrating intellect and the ability to understand complexities and find solutions where others only see confusion and chaos. Greater perceptual sensitivity leads to conscious control of the creative matrix, providing creativity at command. Instinct provides an unerring sense of timing and insight into the nature of human intentions, allowing us to accurately anticipate problems and to know who and when to trust. Intuitive knowledge is the visionary capacity of the mind, bringing insight and the beginnings of true wisdom. But the most powerful of the inner mental resources is an unshakable self-confidence that translates into a powerful will and determination. This confidence is built on inner strength, and finds completion in the mystical experience of the spiritual-Self.

Enlightenment – The Dawning of the Sage

The greatest benefit of a successful meditation practice is the mystical experience of spiritual-Self realization, the conscious awareness of one's eternal Self. With this experience, the warrior begins the spiritual journey that completes the qualities that define the sage. Experiencing the spiritual-Self as his true identity, the warrior gains control of the mind and its resources. Throughout the process, as he gains increasing control over the mind, the warrior becomes more and more fearless. But the final freedom from all fear happens when the warrior achieves a mystical experience, and realizing his own eternal nature, becomes a sage.

Prayer, the path of the heart, refines the ego, and leads to spiritual union with the divine, an experience often referred to as ecstasy, or rapture. It is an experience of being fully loved, accepted, and joined with the God-head. It is the spiritual experience of dualism. On the other hand, meditation, the path of the mind, leads to the experience of unity, the recognition that our essential nature is not the ego-self at all, but the spiritual-Self, a spark of divinity housed in human form. There is no separation between the divinity and one's spiritual-Self. They are one and the same. Instead of ecstasy, the experience is one of unmitigated bliss, an unfathomable joy permeated with tranquility. All striving ends and all loneliness disappears as we experience wholeness. In the Christian tradition, this experience is signified by the phrase "I and my Father are one." This is the undeniable recognition that one's true identity is the divinity itself.

The experience of the spiritual-Self is the diminution of fear and the beginning of genuine wisdom. In the experience of our eternal Self, as a warrior sage we recognize there is no reason to fear anything. Life itself doesn't change, but how we live in that life changes dramatically. The deeply grooved patterns of the mind do not disappear, but they no longer have the power to disturb because personal identity has shifted to the eternal spiritual-Self, no longer tied to the ego-self. Instead of changing the world, we change our presence in the world. In this way, the world changes for the warrior sage.

The Emergence of Will

Meditation leads directly to the emergence of a powerful will. Recall from Chapter 3 that the spiritual principle of will is the power behind the creative thrust of the divine, consisting of the combination of intention and desire. Every spiritual principle has its limited counterpart in the human experience. On an individual level, will translates into genuine confidence and determination. This is the *sankalpa shakti* of tantra philosophy, an inner strength of purpose that cannot be defeated.

What is meant by the term will is not the conflict or struggle indicated by the typical usage of the term "will power." We talk about using will power when we are caught up in a conflict or opposition, either with others or with ourselves. In these situations, we try to over-power resistance, and our energies become focused on the struggle rather than the outcome. When this happens, the energies of the mind are split between the desired goal and the struggle against a competing goal or force. We now bring only half of our power to the achievement of our goal.

Will is a complex quality, consisting of balance, conviction, intention, desire, and confidence. It involves conscious choice, and the ability to marshal and direct all inner resources to achieve a goal. When we use will, we focus all our energy on the goal we wish to achieve. It is an ordering of thought, energy and effort *for* something, rather than *against* something. Obstacles are experienced as just another aspect of the task before us.

The practice of meditation develops the three key aspects of will: a strong foundation, an inner consensus, and effective execution. A strong foundation consists of a balanced mind and body, heightened powers of concentration, and the ability to manage any conflict by remaining calm, clear, and collected. Through self-awareness and spiritual-Self realization, the warrior sage is aware of his inner strength, and creates a personal philosophy consistent with his true nature. His external actions are consistent with his inner thoughts, and this integrity allows him to act in harmony with himself and with the world around him. This leads to an unlimited self-confidence that is based on inner strength and integrity, and not influenced by success or failure. His commitment is based on his integrity and inner strength, and not on others' opinions. The world may not understand the warrior sage, and he may not act in accordance with society's beliefs and values, but he will act in harmony with what is. This allows the warrior sage to act with decisiveness, free from the self-doubts, fears, and worries that plague so many. Being in harmony, his actions are effortless and effective. His discipline allows him to act with freedom, and his deep inner knowledge allows him to act in harmony with effortlessness, ease, and effectiveness.

Meditation: Discipline of the Mind

Meditation is both transformational and transcendental, a process that begins with power and ends with spiritual-Self Realization. There is no other process that is its equal, and it always works. Meditation is a simple event requiring great discipline; it takes time, effort and commitment. Those who say that meditation is easy, or that it is for weak people, or that it is against religious beliefs (and this may be true, but the fault lies in the belief, not in meditation), are ignorant of what meditation actually is: an intentional discipline that leads to complete knowledge and control of the mind, the instrument of knowledge, and opens the door to Self realization.

As the mind is the most powerful tool that we have, it takes great discipline to bring it under direction and control. The warrior sage is unafraid of the word discipline. She recognizes that the achievement of power demands a powerful discipline. Meditating twice a day for fifteen or twenty minutes will not create a warrior sage. This demands a total commitment, where meditation becomes an on-going process. Many are afraid of the word discipline because to them it means that they must force themselves to do something they really don't want to do. The discipline required for meditation has nothing to do with forcing. You cannot force yourself to meditate. You can force yourself to sit, to think about things; but you cannot force yourself to meditate.

As a discipline, meditation is built on curiosity. The warrior sage becomes more and more curious as she explores the various depths, levels, and realities of the mind and spirit. This curiosity is endless, and becomes the single most important driving force for meditation. In this way, discipline means learning to do well what you really want to do. Remember, meditation is effortless concentration, not something forced or compelled. For the warrior sage, meditation becomes a way of life, not something practiced once or twice a day.

We have defined meditation as an internal concentration, but there is also another form of meditation that arises out of the internal focus. Recall that meditation is a process of observation or perception. As such, there are actually two forms of meditation. One is the internal, one-pointed, effortless concentration, discussed above, which leads to an expanded inner awareness and spiritual-Self Realization. The other is an active form, where the entire stream of consciousness becomes the focal point. In tantric yoga, this is referred to as meditation in action and in the Buddhist tradition it is called mindfulness.

Meditation in action leads to greater awareness of both the environment and how the mind is engaging that environment. Instead of observing the subtle flow of a single internal thought, we observe the flow of thought and action, and how our individual thoughts and actions are creating, and are embedded in, the external world. In this way, we become more aware of the situational demands, subtle currents of emotions, intentions, and subtle cause/effect relationships that are part and parcel of our environment. This increased awareness allows the warrior sage to move effectively, particularly during times of pressure when others become confused, disturbed, and stuck. Both forms of meditation are required to achieve the heights of the warrior sage.

Meditation in action leads to enhanced awareness of *now*. We are fully engaged in the present moment, but as an observer rather than as an actor. Being present, engaged in the moment, frees the mind of worry and negativity, allowing us to be fully responsive to the demands of the moment. This is the basis for having peak experiences, those times when we are so focused and engaged that even time seems to stop. Being fully present allows the warrior sage to fully engage the power of discrimination, free from the tyranny of habits that condition the mind. This, of course, leads to greater intuitive knowledge, and he is able to envision the future clearly. Suspending judgment in favor of discrimination, he clearly understands the lessons of the past, learning from mistakes rather than suffering from them.

One final word about meditation – it is very important to find a truly competent teacher. This may prove to be somewhat difficult, but it must be done. The mind is a vast reality, and you can easily become sidetracked in the inner maze of the mind. Reading about meditation and practicing from a book may give you some benefit, but it will be limited. A competent teacher is one who has studied in-depth in a particular discipline, not someone who has visited every famous meditation teacher they could find. It is only through an in-depth study within a particular tradition that meditation can be mastered and the skill gained to teach others.

Through mediation and prayer, we develop the personal and spiritual qualities that characterize the warrior sage. But the job is not yet finished. There is yet one more discipline necessary to complete the journey. We turn now to the discipline of contemplation for the completion of wisdom, and the fulfillment of the sage.

Chapter Seven
Contemplation–The Path to Pure Intelligence

Be still, and know that I am God.
—Psalms 46:10—

The third discipline, contemplation, is the final refinement of intelligence, the mental power of discrimination. Contemplation is the most sophisticated of the three spiritual paths, and requires the most discipline. It is, in many ways, dependent on skills gained in the first two disciplines of prayer and meditation. Prayer provides the freedom from the ego-self through the practice of surrender and the development of humility. As we will see later, it is humility that allows the warrior sage to go beyond the limitations of the beliefs tightly held by the ego-self, and discern the underlying reality, both in the external world and within the spiritual dimension. Meditation provides the focusing power necessary for penetration of the intellect into more and more subtle levels of reality. Without this power and steadiness of focus, contemplation simply degenerates into intellectual masturbation.

To grasp the importance of contemplation, we must understand a little about the structure and functions of the human mind. In an earlier chapter, we briefly explored the function of the ego-self, and saw how the ego-self likes to be in control and pretend that it is the owner.

Subservient to the ego-self is the function of the sensory mind whose purpose is to collect and organize sensory data through the senses. This organization takes place within the field of the mind which provides the contextual background by which interpretation and meaning-making take place. This contextual field includes both short and long-term memory, but is far greater than memory as it provides the entire contextual background out of which we construct a meaningful reality.

The mind itself is not conscious, but it is permeated with Universal Consciousness. Our personal awareness is not a mental process – a thought, feeling, or sensation – at all, but a limited or circumscribed expression of Consciousness as it works through the energy field of the mind. Recall from an earlier discussion that Consciousness is an inherent quality of the divine. In the view of the warrior sage, the fundamental reality is Consciousness, not material phenomenon. Our spiritual-Self is a spark of Consciousness. The spiritual-Self is the source of personal awareness and consciousness, not neural activity or an emergent property of neural activity as posited by materialist philosophers such as Dennett and Searle. For the body to function, and for us to operate in this worldly plane, the brain is a necessary tool. But the absence of the brain does not mean the absence of consciousness; it simply means the absence of the ability to function on this particular material dimension, or plane. Although western science, embedded within a materialist framework, does not recognize or deal with mystical knowledge, experience, or near-death experiences, this does not in any way negate the reality of these experiences or knowledge.

Universal Consciousness is not only pure awareness without an object; it is also pure intelligence and pure power. The spiritual-Self shares these qualities. Just as a drop of ocean water has all the elements of the ocean contained within it, the spiritual-Self has all the awareness, intelligence and power of Consciousness. The spiritual-Self is not the full experience of divinity; it is only a drop, a limited expression of the full experience. But because it is a drop, the spiritual-Self is the portal, the entry into pure awareness, intelligence and power as it permeates the field of mind and becomes the on-board representative of the divine. Embedded within the material field of the mind, the interaction of the spiritual-Self with the mind evolves into the function of discrimination, or *buddhi*. As discussed in the last chapter, discrimination is the capacity to discern reality as it is, to distinguish cause/effect relationships, to recognize or identify distinctness. The function of discrimination is the application of the pure awareness, intelligence, and power that passes through the spiritual-Self. It is the source of knowledge in the mind, as well as the capacity to decide. Illustration 7:1 depicts this relationship.

Thus, the function of discrimination, with the spiritual-Self as its source, is the foundation of intelligence, and consequently knowledge, for the mind. All other functions of the mind, such as the ego-self and the sensory function, arise out of this fundamental capacity. As the illustration shows, Consciousness pervades the entire structure of mind and body, but is more clearly experienced as the mind's energy becomes more subtle and more revealing. This also illustrates that the pure intelligence is beyond the ego.

While the discrimination function engages all other functions, it alone has the capacity to go beyond the limitations of the other functions and discern reality as it actually is. The purity of knowledge that characterizes pure intellect, however, is extremely subtle, making it difficult to engage. It requires both effort and discipline to accomplish. In other words, real thinking is somewhat difficult, and requires balance, focus, awareness, and effort.

Whenever we make a decision, we use the function of discrimination. If, however, we act purely out of habit and do what we have always done, we use only the sensory mind and do not engage the discrimination function. But the moment we pause and reflect, "Should I do this?" or "Should I do that?" we engage discrimination and make a decision about what to do. But there are various degrees to which we access this powerful function. Most of the time, our "thinking" is habitual, subservient to the ego-self, and little to no discrimination is used. Strong beliefs and emotions such as anger, desire, and fear inhibit our capacity to engage discrimination, leading us astray from what is truth at the moment. In other words, we often see, hear and understand what we have learned to see, hear and understand, or even what our emotional reactions dictate to us.

Illustration 7:1

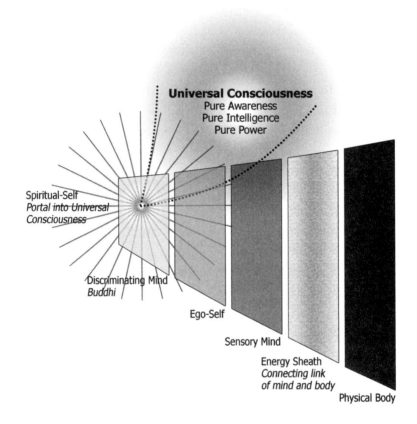

Universal Consciousness
Pure Awareness
Pure Intelligence
Pure Power

Spiritual-Self
*Portal into Universal
Consciousness*

Discriminating Mind
Buddhi

Ego-Self

Sensory Mind

Energy Sheath
*Connecting link
of mind and body*

Physical Body

Thinking, Insight and Intuition

In Chapter 4 we discussed briefly three states of knowledge: critical thinking (analysis), instinct, and intuition. Of these three, instinct is purely perceptual, a non-linear, non-analytic knowledge that is hardwired into the mind/body system. We have the capacity to perceive and know immediately, without thinking about it, what is in our immediate environment that will either hurt or help us (or anyone or anything that we are emotionally identified with, such as our children or our position at work). Through the practice of meditation, we can develop instinctual knowledge to a high degree. Since instinct works through the same pathways as emotional reactions, we often confuse instinctual knowledge with an emotional reaction. Confusing emotional reactions, particularly desires and fears, with instinctual knowledge is the major source of error when trying to utilize instincts. As we gain in self-awareness and self-knowledge through meditation, we minimize this source of error and become skilled in the conscious use of this powerful and helpful knowledge state.

For both intuitive knowledge and critical thinking, the power of discrimination comes into play. Of these two, critical thinking or analysis is far more familiar and common; it is also far more problematic and error-prone than the other two states of knowledge. The reason for this is that critical thinking is subject/object knowledge. There is a knower, a process of knowing, and the known object. The relationship between subject and object relationship is defined by the process of knowing. This, in turn, is determined by the particular perspective that we bring to the task. The perspective we bring largely determines the answers we derive. In other words, our beliefs (perspective) largely determine the answers we come up with.

For example, I can understand a world event from the perspective of an American, a European, or an African; I can look at the event from the point of view of a particular religion, a certain academic discipline, from a humanitarian point of view, even from the point of view of a disinterested observer. It is not only possible, but very probable, that I will have a very different view of the same event. Not only is understanding determined by the perspective we have, our beliefs even determine what we may physically see or hear. (Perspective does not play a significant role in true instinctual knowledge, but does play a key role in structuring emotional reactions).

One of the greatest problems we face is the inability to think "outside the box." To do this we must step outside our own limiting beliefs (perspective) and think in new ways, see different possibilities, and find creative or innovative answers. The more strongly we hold on to a belief, the more difficult it is to step outside the box of that belief. Unfortunately, our thoughts are as strongly conditioned as our behaviors. Habits are hard to break, whether it is smoking or thinking in the same old way. Such common phrases as "this is the way we always do it" and "not invented here" or "we have to follow the rules" reflect the pervasive power of habitual belief to interfere with effective and innovative critical thinking.

Even more powerful are the paradigms that rule our thinking. Paradigms are coherent belief systems, such as classical physics, psychoanalysis, or quantum mechanics. Words that end with the suffix of "-ism", such as communism, Catholicism, socialism, capitalism, often indicate a paradigm, a coherent body of thought or beliefs. Academic disciplines, religions, medicine, even cultures are ruled by paradigms. Often these paradigms are elevated to the level of "truth" and become entrenched in the mind. When paradigms become entrenched, they dominate thinking patterns, inhibit creativity and innovation, and typically lead to the same old conclusions. Often any deviation from "the truth" is strongly discouraged, in fact even punished. The old adage that "Science precedes death by death" reflects the power of ingrained belief systems to limit understanding, creativity, and progress.

Beliefs are powerful and useful tools of the mind. They provide a framework for moving effectively in the world. But beliefs are nothing more than hypotheses of reality, and must constantly be tested with direct experience, insights, and new learning. When beliefs are elevated to the level of "truth," personal growth stops, and learning comes to an end. When belief systems become enthroned as truth, one-way thinking arises and grows into fanaticism, and the individual lives in an ever smaller landscape, becoming more fearful and rigid as he desperately clings to his increasingly dysfunctional beliefs.

Maintaining an observer stance to his own thoughts, the warrior sage is able to challenge his own belief systems, always testing these hypotheses in the laboratory of direct experience. Having the freedom to challenge his own beliefs, he remains flexible, innovative and creative. He uses beliefs as a tool to enhance understanding, and to guide his explorations. But he is always ready to alter beliefs in the face of direct evidence and experience. In this way, the warrior sage continues to grow and develop in both knowledge and wisdom.

Emotional reactions and states are another serious source of error for critical thinking. When we are out of balance emotionally, it colors every thought we have. The more disturbed we are, the less clearly we can think about anything. Of course, the quality and/or quantity of information can seriously impact the quality of our critical thinking, but in effective decision making, information often turns out to be far less important than beliefs (perspective) and emotions.

To help refine the process, we turn to logic in order to minimize error. But logical systems cannot determine the truth of anything; they only serve to minimize error. Different logical systems can even arrive at different answers, but again, we are back to the issue of perspective. This is not to say that we should not use logic, only that it is one part of the process, and certainly not the most critical element. Emotions and beliefs can quickly interfere with any system of logic. Even worse, logic is often used to justify emotional positions. We often use our creative intelligence to find creative ways to destroy our enemies, and ultimately, ourselves. The continual sophistication and proliferation of weapons systems is a clear example of how logic and intelligence can be enslaved by emotion.

Discrimination: Entry into Intelligence

The power of the discrimination function lies in its relationship to the spiritual-Self, the portal into pure intelligence. While we use discrimination in conjunction with the sensory mind when we reason, or engage critical thinking, the discrimination function is superior to the sensory function, and is not subject to the same limitations found in the sensory mind. The power of discrimination lies in the fact that it is not restricted by time/space or pain/pleasure, two powerful limitations embedded within the sensory function that play a key role in the organization of sensory data.

Knowledge derived purely from the discrimination function, however, is not based on subject/object knowledge, but rather knowledge based on identity with the object. In yoga science, this is described as the mind going out to the object. The term "identity" indicates that the mind and the object become one and the same, without the mediating effects of time/space or pain/pleasure In other words, we gain direct knowledge without the limits imposed by learning or habit. While a detailed discussion of this process of knowledge formation is beyond the scope of this book, a brief description of this knowledge base is necessary to see why this is central to the warrior sage.

Both mind and material objects are forms of energy. For example, a chair and the thought of the chair are both forms of energy. On the sensory level, if I look at a chair and think about it, there is a gulf between my thought of the chair and the chair itself. There is a subject/object relationship mediated by the particular perspective (beliefs, attitudes, esthetic judgments, etc.) that determine how I think about the chair. My thought of the chair and the chair are usually considered to be absolutely different and separate from each other. In Western thought, there is a fundamental and unbridgeable gulf between the subjective experience of my thought about the chair and the material reality of the chair.

However, from a yogic perspective, this experience of separateness and difference is an emergent quality, not a fundamental reality. It is a consequence of the how the sensory mind and ego-self work together to create individuality and difference, and to locate objects in space and time.

Through the senses and the sensory mind, we experience the material world as solid, as a gross form of energy. However, elementary physics tells us that what appears as solid at another level is actually a bound form (gross level) of energy. The underlying reality is that the chair is not really solid; it only appears that way to our senses. If we were to take a powerful electron microscope, we would find that the chair actually consists of all sorts of atomic particles, which in turn, are nothing more than forms of energy. What appears in the macroscopic level as solid is actually a bound form of energy. The most fundamental level of reality, even beyond that of chemistry, is energy. There is nothing new or surprising here, and this fact, that the fundamental reality of the entire material world is energy, is taught in high school physics.

This normally has little relevance for day-to-day life as we go through the day acting as if everything really is as solid as our senses tell us. But within the material structure of the mind, at the level of discrimination, a very different event happens. Both the chair and the thought are experienced as forms of energy. At the most subtle level of mind, the energy of the mind has the capacity to model the energy form of any object. In other words, the mind and the object become identical, and knowledge is from the inside out rather than from the outside in as we find in analytic or critical thinking. The profound philosophical implications of this statement are beyond the scope of this book, but in a very real way, we literally participate in creating the reality in which we function.

One way to understand this is to think about how we share a program from our computer with a friend who has a different computer. Let's say that you have a wonderful game that you are willing to share with me. You put a CD into the computer and copy the game on to the CD, and mail it to me. I get the CD, put it into my computer, and copy the game into my computer. Now you and I have the exactly the same game. What essentially happened is that my computer now has the identical magnetic field with identical characteristics, and so we have the same outcomes. I didn't copy a bunch of words, pictures and logical rules; these were all contained in the magnetic field. Once the identical field is established, the outcomes are the same.

This is analogous to what happens within the discriminating function. At this most subtle level of the mind, the energy field of the mind becomes identical with the energy field of the object (person, place, thing, or concept). The information embedded in the field of the object is now embedded within the energy field of the mind. As the discriminating mind creates the same energy field pattern, it now has access to all this information. Another way of saying this is that as we become more focused, and create a more intense, concentrated neurological field, we are able to penetrate the embedded information within the energy field of the object. In this way, the object is known from the inside out, and perspective has little to no relevance.

The knowledge gained in this way is pure, unbiased, and identical. It is free of the biases that limit the sensory mind, such as time/space, emotions, habits, beliefs, and perspectives. This is not a perceptual process as we normally think of it, as the sensory mind and its mechanisms are not involved. Rather, it is a process of discernment, of direct apperception or recognition at the most subtle levels of material reality. We don't create or develop this fundamental level of knowing, it already exists. This emergence of knowledge arises from Consciousness, the pure awareness, intelligence, and power that gives birth to all manifestation. A more prosaic way of saying this is that all knowledge (omniscience) already exists within the divine, and the function of discrimination is the power tool by which we as individual selves approach this knowledge.

The knowledge itself is not the variable, it already exists. As discussed earlier, Newton did not "discover" gravity and the laws that govern it; he became aware of the reality that already existed. Because of his increased awareness, others were able to become aware of the same reality. The variable is the degree of our personal awareness, our ability to tap into this knowledge. The process of discrimination is graduated, or progressive, depending on several factors. Our ability to access and use discrimination depends primarily on three factors: our capacity to focus attention, the clarity, depth and breadth of our awareness, and our ability to witness without bias.

This process of gaining knowledge through identity is not as strange as it might seem. We all engage identity knowledge from the very beginning. The term that may be more familiar is modeling, the most powerful form of learning, and the most impactful. As children, we model our parents, and end up very much like them. Anyone with children eventually realizes that the child doesn't become what you want them to be, they become who you are. After all, the apple doesn't fall far from the tree. In many ways, we become our parents because of modeling, or identity knowledge.

The same principle operates when an aspiring athlete watches a top performer, and then visualizes himself performing exactly as he saw the expert perform. He is modeling himself after the skilled athlete first in his thought or visualization, and that translates into more effective performance for his body. Visualization, or mental modeling, is recognized as one of the more powerful ways to enhance performance. And all visualization is essentially a modeling process.

Judging vs. Discrimination

Another familiar experience of this discriminative knowledge is our conscience. Genuine conscience is not the habitual value judgments of good and bad that we learn from parents, teachers, preachers, and other regulators of our development, but rather the power to know what is helpful or beneficial to us and what is not helpful or beneficial. It is that still, quiet voice that we sometimes hear, but often don't listen to. The real voice of our conscience is quiet and soft, while the voice of fears, wants, and desires is noisy and loud. The false conscience, or what Freud called the super-ego, is loud and accusatory, and is nothing more than rantings of an ego-self enslaved with the habits of guilt learned from the policemen of our childhood. More than one sage has told us to listen to the "still, small voice" if we want to make the right choices for ourselves.

When we judge something, we evaluate it according to some standard, such as which is bigger, stronger, brighter, and so on. Standards are both arbitrary and learned, decided by a culture, a particular tradition, or a belief system. It doesn't matter how many may agree with any particular standard; it is still arbitrary. When we judge something better than something else, we are deciding on the basis of our perspective. This is how we create organization, make laws, and even do science. In science this arbitrary agreement is called consensual validation, and is a key element in scientific exploration, theory building, and progress. Success in any endeavor depends on one's ability to make effective judgments.

Much of what we evaluate or judge, particularly physical designators, such as size, color, strength, or density, are generally well defined, and consequently, have strong consensual validation, so there is little argument about the judgment. However, things become much more problematic when dealing with values, particularly those which evoke emotionally loaded terms, such as right and wrong, good and bad, beautiful or ugly, or desirable or undesirable. Value judgments are, more often than not, the source of conflict and disagreement, particularly amongst different groups of people. A well-known saying goes, "beauty is in the eyes of the beholder," but this is often forgotten when beliefs are held as truth. Not only is beauty arbitrary, so is good and bad, right and wrong, and a whole host of judgmental terms. Value judgments are the source of a great deal of drama, and the result is clouded thinking, poor decision-making, and difficult relationships.

Rather than making judgments, the warrior sage refines her power of discrimination in order to make decisions based on cause/effect relationships rather than on arbitrary standards. Good and bad are really irrelevant concepts when cause/effect becomes the basis for decision-making. This way the warrior sage avoids drama and stays with the data of the situation for maintaining clarity of thought and effective decision making.

Intuition: Discrimination as Recognition

Although discrimination is the basis for rational analysis, it is not an analytic process. Pure discrimination is a process of discernment, or illumination. It is, ultimately, the creative process where thought begins, and as such, is the foundation of all personal reality. Through discrimination, we have direct apprehension of "what is', without the limiting impact of time/space or pain/pleasure. This knowledge is not limited to the present moment.

The knowledge gained from pure discrimination is called intuition. When we focus attention inward, we can gradually gain awareness of the spiritual-Self, and access its power and resources. This leads to the mystical experience, the direct experience of Consciousness. When we focus attention on the material reality, we can become aware of the subtle cause/effect relationships that determine so-called "future" consequences. With intuition, we experience the reality as it actually exists rather than how we have learned to see it as dictated by our habits. Free from the restrictions of time and space, we clearly see and understand the inevitable consequences of these cause/effect relationships.

Pure intuitive knowledge is also free from the errors created by perspective and emotional influences. The difficulty in utilizing intuition is not because of some error, but developing the inner awareness necessary to access this most subtle level of the mind. It happens occasionally to everyone, such as the above example concerning our conscience. We really do know what choices to make, we do have insight into consequences, we do know the decision we must make. Through discrimination, the human mind is incredibly visionary. The problem lies in the fact that we don't have the requisite level of skill, the refined conscious ability, to access this level of knowledge whenever we choose. Since our educational system rarely, if ever, provides the inner training necessary to become a skilled human being, we are left to whatever haphazard opportunities happen along the way.

The warrior sage does not leave this powerful resource, or any other, to chance. The discriminative function is the access to pure intelligence, and as such, is the access to power, knowledge and wisdom. As in all inner resources, the warrior sage embarks on a systematic self-training program to refine this powerful resource to the level of conscious skill. This systematic discipline is the path of contemplation.

Contemplation: The Path of Intelligence

The discipline of contemplation is the refinement of discrimination and the access to pure intelligence, awareness, and power. Contemplation is the process by which we refine the power of discrimination to such a degree that every truth, be it large or small, becomes a direct experience. The act of contemplation involves objective observation and rigorous discrimination. Nothing is accepted as a given truth or irrevocable fact. The process is one of discerning relationships, not reaching conclusions. Good and bad become irrelevant; judgment is recognized as a trap for the mind. Categories are seen as temporary shelters, constructed only to facilitate further observation. In contemplation, the knowledge processes of the mind remain fluid, probing deeper and deeper into the nature of ideas, concepts, things, and actions. Contemplation is not only thinking about something, but also focusing the whole mind, all attention, on the object of study. Our whole being – emotions, thoughts, actions – becomes involved.

The task is to bring the most powerful learning process of the mind, that of modeling, or knowledge through identity, under our conscious control. It is the culmination of the disciplines of prayer and meditation, the final step leading to the fulfillment of wisdom, the completion of knowledge, and the direct experience of Universal Consciousness. In the highest traditions of yoga science, contemplation is considered to be the queen of all spiritual disciplines.

This is reflected in the following story:

A great and holy man had lived his life dedicated to the will of God. He became so filled with grace that any prayer he uttered was immediately fulfilled. His heart was generous and kind, and he was a great inspiration to all who knew him. As he grew in the Spirit, his knowledge and wisdom became legendary. And when he died, many grieved at the loss of such a great person. At the time of his passing, he entered the gates of Heaven and knocked at the door of God's house.

"Who is there?" demanded God

"It is I, thy faithful servant," responded the holy man.

"Oh yes, my beloved child, I am overjoyed to see you," replied God. "You have done very well, and I am pleased with you. But there is still some work to be done. Please return for another life and continue your great work."

The great man was reborn and again spent an exemplary life, becoming even wiser and more enlightened than before. Through prayer and meditation, he gained such clarity of mind that he could explain the most profound scriptures in such simple terms and with such clarity that even the simplest would gain insight. His love for God and others was so immense that his name became synonymous with the word "love." All who came into his presence experienced a profound change of heart. Enemies would become friends, criminals would turn to charitable works, and those in distress would find peace and harmony. Finally, the great sage again passed from the physical plane, and it seemed that the entire world grieved for his passing. Approaching the house of God, he knocked again at the door.

"Who is there?" asked God.

"It is I, thy faithful servant," cried the great sage.

"Oh yes, my beloved son, I am pleased with you and overjoyed to see you," said God. "But still, there is some work you must do. Please return for another life and continue your wonderful work."

Again, the sage returned to be reborn. In this lifetime the sage, along with prayer and meditation, began to ponder the great truths of his insights and experiences. He began to realize that everywhere he looked everything he saw was only another manifestation of the Divine Will. He saw God in the murderer as well as the saint, in the storm as well as in the sunset, in each creature and every rock. Contradictions and dualities resolved themselves in the power of his discrimination, imperfections dissolved in the power of his vision, and conflicts disappeared in the power of his love. With absolute clarity, he saw there was only one Realty – that God alone existed. What he had previously seen as good and bad, as desirable and undesirable, as holy and unholy, was all nothing more than another manifestation of the Divine Will. Some who knew him hated him, some loved him, and most were unaware of his existence. He saw all equally with a calm, clear and undisturbed mind and vision. When he passed from this life, only a fortunate few disciples knew what loss had taken place.

At this passing, when he arrived at God's home, again he knocked at the door.

"Who is there?" demanded God.

"Thine Own Self," replied the sage.

"Enter and be welcome, my beloved," replied God.

Through contemplation, the warrior sage enters the realm of creative will and universal knowledge, developing the visionary skills, wisdom and compassion that characterize the qualities of the sage. Through contemplation, with the refinement of prayer and meditation, the journey is successful, and the destiny of the warrior sage is fulfilled.

But to master contemplation is a daunting task; it requires developing mastery over the most subtle levels of the mind and its resources. To accomplish this requires discipline and commitment, as well as enhanced skills with both prayer and meditation. We must have the power to focus without distraction, the ability to step out of the box of our own beliefs and perspectives, and the awareness and clarity of the most subtle quantum realms of the mind where knowledge fields are penetrated and personal reality is first formed.

Prayer and Meditation: The Foundation

Once we understand the roles that emotions, beliefs, and perspectives play in critical thinking, it becomes apparent that both prayer and meditation play a central role in the discipline of contemplation. Recall that the discipline of prayer is essentially the discipline of surrender. From this arises humility, which becomes a powerful tool in the discipline of contemplation. It is through surrender that the warrior sage finds the way to free herself from the tyranny of belief. Humility allows her to step away from the limitations of the ego-self with its attendant needs, desires, wants, and fears. This is critical because contemplation demands that we step away from the habits of thought, away from the ideas, concepts, and beliefs that normally frame the thinking process.

We seldom realize the degree that past learning limits the way that we think about things. Innovative thinking, creative problem solving, and the realization of deeper realities and truths all demand that we step "outside the box" that normally frames our thinking. Without humility, contemplation remains simply a refinement of "more of the same." Logic becomes dominant, and progress along the same lines is assured. Instead of real change, we simply find ways to do what we already do, but only better.

There are all too many examples of ego-driven belief systems where "more of the same" dominates: politics, religion, the inability to truly make peace (but we do make better weapon systems), even the health-care crisis (but we can use better technology, define best practices for treating disease, and refine insurance policies). So-called "thought-leaders" simply offer more of the same, only better. There is rarely true innovation, only refinement and insignificant insights along the edges of our beloved paradigms. Without humility, beliefs (perspectives and paradigms) become "truth" instead of tools, and we hold on to ever-smaller realities, leading to even greater problems than before.

To those who have not developed genuine humility, it seems like a great sacrifice to surrender all attachments to the ego-self and move beyond the limiting paradigms of one's established thought patterns. But it is only by stepping away from habitual patterns of thinking and being that we are able to respond creatively and spontaneously to the demands that we face. Otherwise, we continue to do what we have always done, and get the same results that we have always gotten.

This process is not a matter of using logic. Although logic is essential in the early stages of contemplation, the discipline itself goes far beyond any system of logic. Logic, a powerful tool to minimize error, is necessarily limited by the perspective with which one begins. In contemplation, you must transcend perspective in order to realize truth. Ultimately, one has to completely give up all judgment in order to see the reality which is beyond standards, expectations, and evaluations.

Genuine humility allows the warrior sage the freedom to step away from his own beliefs and perspectives, to "walk in the shoes of the other" and accept other points of view as valid. He moves freely in the realm of data, avoiding the drama that drives the ego-self and drastically limits creative thought. Giving up the need to be "right" allows him to indulge "radical" ways of thought and action. The consequences of humility for the warrior sage are spontaneity, creativity, and insight. Rather than sacrifice, we are stepping into freedom.

The discipline of meditation provides other key elements to the discipline of contemplation. Along with the direct knowledge (experience) of the spiritual-Self, meditation develops power through refined concentration skills. Concentration provides three key elements of contemplation: calmness, clarity, and depth. Research from all over the world consistently proves that those who practice meditation develop a greater calmness of mind, a greater emotional stability (less anger and fear), and stabilize all the physiological and psychological parameters involved with stress. A relaxed, calm, mind is absolutely essential for the practice of contemplation.

Emotional disturbance, compulsive thoughts, desires, and wants all interfere with the ability to think clearly and effectively. Under stress, the mind becomes more and more locked into habitual patterns, negating any effort to think outside the box, or even to think clearly within the box. Distraction is a great enemy of effective thought, and this is particularly true of contemplation. Without the ability to focus clearly and calmly, the mind constantly reacts to any distraction from the senses or from the bed of memory. The greater the emotional reactivity, the more difficult it is to think clearly and in depth about any topic. As the mind/body complex and the ego-self become more stable, not only does the quality of thought increase, but the warrior sage is able to sustain a line of thought more consistently and effortlessly, leading to greater penetration of the knowledge field and thus creating a greater depth of understanding.

Illustration 7:2

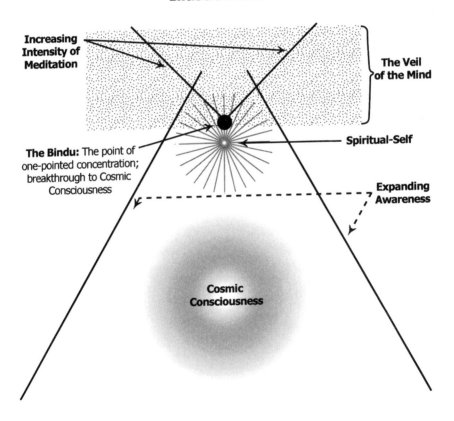

The most important contribution to contemplation, however, is the expansion of awareness, shown in Illustration 7:2. Here again, meditation plays a key role. In the creative process of knowledge formation, the greater the ability to concentrate, the greater the ability to penetrate into the subtle knowledge fields in the quantum levels of the mind. It is a matter of expanding awareness into the greater field of consciousness. Recall from our discussion in Chapter 6, that the greater the concentration, the greater the awareness. Even on a physical level, the greater our ability to concentrate, the more consistent the neural field. The more consistent the neural field, the greater the ability to expand awareness into the more subtle fields of the mind. The outcome for the warrior sage is greater insight and wisdom. It is this expansion of personal consciousness into the ever-present field of consciousness that is the goal of contemplation.

Stillness: Key to Inner Awareness

Key to the successful practice of contemplation is the simplest of all demands – the ability to become still. The simplest task, however, is often the most difficult. This seems to be particularly true for stillness. For most, achieving stillness is an excruciating exercise in futility. We are a culture of constant movement and stimulation. Sadly, few perceive the power and value of stillness, but stillness allows the more subtle levels of the mind to rise into awareness, bringing insight and wisdom to our conscious awareness.

Stillness exists at several levels, beginning with physical stillness and ending with a deep inner stillness that merges into profound silence. At each level, there are benefits to be gained from the stillness. Stillness at the physical level leads to insight and problem solving. For example, one of the most effective ways to solve a difficult problem is to sit absolutely still for sixty minutes. This is not a meditation exercise, and the mind does not need to be one-pointed or focused. In fact, in the early stages of contemplation, thoughts are not rigidly directed or controlled at all, but instead, allowed to flow freely and creatively. The body is held very still, with only essential movements, such as breathing and blinking, allowed.

Physical stillness is only the first step. Eventually, through the practice of physical stillness, we become aware of an inner stillness, a quality of the spiritual-Self. This inner stillness is dynamic, expanding and effortless. Through practice, the warrior sage is able to enter this dynamic stillness, and still be physically moving. Another way to achieve this inner stillness is through the skilled practice of the Chinese martial art of Taiji Quan.

It is in this inner stillness that contemplation is practiced. It is in stillness that we witness and experience the formation of knowledge within the faculty of discrimination. Inner stillness allows the warrior sage to experience the process of knowing, and thus experience the necessary link between the knower and the known, or in more common parlance, to experience the relationship between subject and object. It is the process of knowing, the actual formation of knowledge itself, that defines contemplation. All relational aspects of any one thought are clearly evident, and the essential meaning of the object is experienced directly. In other words, the knower (consciousness, the witness), the known (the object of contemplation) and the process of knowing (the discriminative function of the mind) become one.

As in all disciplines, the degree of skill determines the quality and extent of the knowledge acquired. The outcome of any discipline is dependent on the skill of the practitioner. The same is true with the spiritual disciplines of prayer, meditation, and contemplation. Contemplation may be used for material issues, such as solving complex problems, gaining visionary insights, or resolving personal issues. Contemplation, like prayer and meditation, becomes a practical tool for the warrior sage, providing insight, vision and clarity to the problems and challenges of everyday life. This is, of course, the foundation for truly effective leadership.

The greatest benefit of contemplation, however, is the fulfillment of spiritual realization. Both prayer and meditation lead to significant spiritual insights and experiences, but it is contemplation that completes the journey of transformation and transcendence. It is through contemplation that the warrior sage goes beyond all belief, all names, all forms, and experiences the fullness of divinity directly. He experiences the underlying unity of all life and becomes fully human. In all great spiritual traditions of contemplation, all thoughts, beliefs, and labels of divinity are eventually discarded. In the Vedic tradition, this is known as the philosophy of negation – *nyeti, nyeti, nyeti* – meaning "not this, not this, not this." Contemplation becomes so refined that it finally leads one to recognize that even the names of God are only names. As a great yogi sage once said, "I had to take my sword and slay the Divine Mother." The sword was the power of discrimination; the Divine Mother was his concept of divinity, his belief in God. Through contemplation, the great sage realized that his belief of God was not God, only a belief. Only by giving up the belief, which was the ultimate "false idol," was he able to realize the actuality of God through direct experience.

By gaining this final goal, the warrior sage achieves the perfection of compassion and equanimity, the defining qualities of the sage. It is the union of perfect knowledge and perfect love. Wherever he looks, he sees and experiences divinity, and becomes the complete mystic. The warrior sage mystic does not live for God, the mystic lives inside of God. The warrior sage lives and experiences all the varieties of life, ups and downs, pain and pleasure, joys and sorrows, but remains undisturbed by them, seeing them as they truly are, part of the infinite variety of the expressions of the divine. All polarities are resolved, and all events are understood in the light of his full consciousness.

As the great mystic poet, T.S. Eliot pointed out in the last poetry he wrote, in the end, there is always a beginning. There is no time in infinity, no beginning and no ending, and the journey is never finished. For the warrior sage, there is no goal to complete, nothing to become, and no crowning achievement to reach, only the realization of the process itself. This realization is the fulfillment of our human destiny. Our human destiny has many beginnings and many endings, but the spiritual-Self, the on-board representative of divinity, does not suffer beginnings and endings. We are sojourners in the great play of the divine, and this human expression is the playground. But we should not confuse the playground with the dancer. It is not the goal of the warrior sage to finish a journey, but to realize that he is the process itself. It's when we learn to dance that we become a warrior sage.

Chapter Eight
Transformation—Engaging a Journey

Never trust a monk who doesn't dance.
—*Zen Saying*—

So what is it like to take the journey? We are already on it. Life is the journey, and it has been going on forever. A human being is the mediating point between matter and spirit, the Creator and the created, and the intersection of time and timelessness in the journey of life. Most people are so caught up in the external demands and distractions – the pleasures and pains – of daily life that they are unaware that a journey even exists. Being unaware of their own power, they become victims of the journey, clinging to some vague hope of future redemption, ease, and reward, or struggle valiantly to accumulate as much happiness as they can eke out of this life in whatever ways seem most important – seeking as much fame, power, wealth, and material possessions as possible. All is a vain effort to satisfy the endless needs, fears, and desires of the ego-self.

The great sages of all traditions tell us that we are asleep, unaware that the Kingdom of Heaven is right before us. With little or no awareness of the spiritual-Self and the immensity within, we desperately cling to materialism in our science, our religions, and our life-style. We experience life as a struggle to overcome fears and loneliness, engaging in a constant search for pleasure, and a futile attempt to avoid pain. All the while, we distract ourselves with whatever we can – drugs, wealth, fame, week-end sports, and the ever-growing stimulation of i-pods, mobile phones, and the internet. The outcome of this materialism is ennui, isolation, and dis-ease, leading to decreasing mental and physical well-being.

The difference between the warrior sage and others is that the warrior sage recognizes that she is the meeting point, and becomes skilled in the integration of matter and spirit. To engage life as a warrior sage we must explore our inner reality and become as skilled with our inner resources as we are in using the resources of the external world. The "journey" of a warrior sage begins with the advent of inner awareness, a turning inward to explore the resources and processes that literally, and ultimately, are the source of the reality in which we live.

This is a journey without a destination because we are already living within the divine. There is nothing to achieve because we are already everything we need. There is no one to compete against because beyond the uniqueness of each mind/body complex, through the portal of the individual spiritual-Self, we are all expressions of the same source. This is not a journey of competition, achievement, and acquisition, but a journey of attention, awareness and expansion.

We can liken this to what appears to be the largest living organism on the planet, a grove of aspen trees located in the Western United States. Aspen trees are unique in that several trees will grow out of the same root system. This particular grove is very large, consisting of hundreds of trees. The trees appear to be individuals in a large forest, but in reality, it is one living organism. Each tree grows out of a single root system that exists below the surface. Each leaf on every tree is part of the same underlying unity. Even though they appear to be unique individual leaves, they are really just manifestations of a greater underlying reality. And this reality is very different from the appearance.

We like to think of ourselves as unique individuals, separate from all others, and certainly different and separate from other life forms. We may share similar backgrounds, beliefs, culture, and so forth, but we really appear to be separate, just like the leaves on the aspen trees. When the wind blows, we rub up against each other, sometimes in pleasant ways, and sometimes in destructive ways. But in all ways, we experience ourselves as separate. And certainly, each human being, each expression of the life force, is a unique expression; and that uniqueness provides a wonderful enrichment of life.

But like the individual and unique leaves of the aspen grove, our hidden, underlying reality is quite different. While most of us are content believing that we are individual leaves, we are really only a small part of a much greater reality. More thoughtful individuals will associate the branch of the tree as the nation or culture that we live in, and see the tree itself as representing humanity. They may also see the other trees as representing other life forms, but the truth lies in the root system. We really aren't the leaves, the branches, the tree itself, or even the root system that joins all the trees. We are really the life force within the root system that permeates the entire grove, or in our case, the entire universe. It is this subtle reality that is the focus for the journey of the warrior sage.

Being vs. Becoming

What is critical is the attitude and perspective by which we take this journey. The perspective of the warrior sage is not of some deficit to fix, but rather one of fully recognizing the divinity that lies within the heart of who we are, and the power that already exists because of this inherent divinity. In truth, we are spiritual beings, and we are here to have a human experience. It is not a question of becoming holy or spiritual, because we already are. We don't have to become intelligent, because intelligence is the source of who we are. Our only task is to overcome our ignorance of the power and intelligence at all levels – body, mind, and spirit – that we are provided with to take this journey. All journeys are spiritual journeys because all beings are spiritual beings. The goal of the warrior sage is to become fully conscious, to be aware of the powerful inner resources of the body, mind, and spirit, to realize the full potential of our humanity.

This makes the journey very different from the pop-psychology self-help culture of continuous self-improvement, and the competitive

"striving to achieve" mentality so characteristic of modern materialism and corporate culture. There is no competition in this journey, and
there is no striving. It is not a matter of becoming better than who you
are. The core problem is ignorance, or lack of awareness. The task is
simply one of recognition: becoming aware of the powerful resources
of the total human, body, mind, and spirit that already exist, and once
aware, developing these powerful resources as conscious skills. The
journey of the warrior sage is a unique process of engagement. There
is really no place to go and nothing to achieve. At the same time, it requires enormous discipline, commitment, and attention.

"Hold on!" you say. "This creates a bit of a conundrum. If there
is no place to go and nothing to achieve, but it takes enormous discipline, commitment, and attention, this is at the least confusing and
contradictory. What is going on here?"

Here's the key. The warrior sage journey is an organic, evolutionary process. This means that it is a growth process that manifests
change naturally from the inside-out. Engaging the journey of a warrior sage is above and beyond everything else a matter of attention, of
being present in the moment, and not creating drama. To accomplish
this requires that we engage a number of different practices in order to
refine awareness, develop our capacity to witness, and refine our power
of concentration. But it is essential to understand that the word practice
means exactly that, not an exercise in perfection or striving to be perfect. The process is one of effortless effort. Instead of going to work on
ourselves, we teach ourselves to dance.

And There is Only the Dance

To dance means to express yourself as freely and as skillfully as
you can. Any skill is the consequence of a disciplined practice. Since our
task is to become a skilled human being, the only requirement is that we
practice the tools and techniques that lead to this outcome. This includes
the physical and mental tools and practices defined in Chapter 4, but
more critically, the spiritual disciplines of prayer, meditation, and contemplation. The practice of spiritual disciplines brings about an organic
change, a change that occurs from within, naturally and spontaneously.

This avoids the emotional conflict and dramas created when we negatively judge ourselves as not being "good enough" or incomplete, and try somehow to be "better," more spiritual, or more insightful. In yoga there is a saying that unhelpful and destructive behaviors, thoughts, and feelings drop away like ripe fruit off a tree. There is no pressure to be different, to be better, or to change into something different. The only demand is to engage the journey to the best of your ability. The engagement for the warrior sage is a dance with herself, not an effort to become pure according to some external and arbitrary standard.

There are unlimited numbers of "authorities" telling you what you should do and who you should be. Worse is the belief of many religions that man is inherently evil and suffers from original sin. This unhealthy belief confuses the ego-self with the true spiritual-Self, and actually is a subtle denial of divinity as the only foundation and source of all life. After all, if God is everywhere, then he must be in the human as well. The moment you think you must change yourself, you create a tension within yourself, a dis-ease and dis-harmony that leads to dysfunction and pain, and interferes with personal growth and development. You begin to strive either for something that isn't present, or judge something present as unacceptable. In short, you are trying to "change" the reality that exists because it doesn't fit some pre-ordained criteria. You are not "good enough," or you need to be "better," or "different," or whatever the criteria demands.

The perspective of the warrior sage is very different: at the most subtle level of our being, we are already in harmony. Our true identity is the spiritual-Self, the on-board representative of the divine. The problem lies in that we aren't aware of that divinity within. So instead of experiencing the harmony of our spiritual being, we identify with the conflicts and disharmony generated by the habits of our mind. We constantly strive to be better, be more competent, and make more money —to somehow improve our condition. The striving itself leads to unlimited misery and unhappiness. The judgments we make about ourselves create even further unhappiness, neuroticism, and fears. As the old comic strip character Pogo once stated, "We have found the enemy and it is us!"

The journey of the warrior sage is one of acceptance, not approval or disapproval. What is there to approve or disapprove of in God? Religions, invested in the need to control, set up the concept of sin with the promise of redemption if you behave in a certain way. But if there is no sin, there is no need for redemption, and there is no need for control. The only control that is genuinely meaningful is self-control, or as Ghandi called it, swaraj, which arises out of self-discipline. The need is not for more laws and rules, but for a greater awareness of the divinity within, the purity that already exists. Of course, wrong-doing, harming others, evil, and all the stupid and dreadful things humans do to each other do exist. These are nothing more than stupid human tricks, done through and by ignorance. The solution has never been, and will never be, controlling others through fear, intimidation, rules, and laws. In the final chapter, we shall return to the problem of good and evil, morality, and laws. As we will see later, for the warrior sage, these and other social conventions have little relevance.

What is totally relevant is developing awareness of the inner strength and wisdom that characterize the foundation of our being. This is achieved primarily through the practice of spiritual disciplines, but also involves utilizing the relevant tools for the mind and body. Rather than a learning process, we can understand it more clearly as an unlearning process, a letting go of all the limitations with which we identify. This is the practice of non-attachment, both to the fruits (consequences) of our actions, but also to the concepts, habits, and patterns that structure our personal ego-self identity.

We all begin with the drive to become perfect, to be better, and to grow as individuals. The practices gradually lead to a far more powerful force that allows us to let go of striving, and to be free of the need to change. This force is the most subtle, yet the most powerful of all desires, and that is the desire for higher knowledge, for the return to our spiritual source. We first experience this desire as curiosity.

The Grace of Curiosity

Those who study neurobiology will tell you that the human brain is designed to learn. More importantly, it retains that capacity for learning throughout life. It isn't true that you can't teach an old dog new tricks; we never lose our capacity to learn. More importantly, we can never lose the desire for higher knowledge, and we will always retain our curiosity. The problem lies in the fact that curiosity is often buried beneath the demands of life. One of the most damaging influences to curiosity is the demand for uniformity, that everyone be the same, that we all believe the same, that we all think the same, that we all live within the rules, mores, laws, and other restrictions so favored by the control freaks of education, religion, government, society, and corporations. Monolithic institutions are inevitably destructive to the expression of curiosity, and consequently, are deadly to the growth and development of every individual.

One of the most prevalent ways that we bury curiosity is "either/or" thinking, such as "you are either for us or against us," "you either support the war or you support terrorists," "you either give me the 'right answer' or you fail," "you are either a Christian or you will go to hell." A well-known example is the Taliban, the primitive, uneducated religious fanatics who controlled Afghanistan for several years. These backward, destructive, and narrow-minded religious fanatics demanded one-way, either/or thinking. The outcome was a degeneration of the entire Afghan culture and way of life.

We find the same pressures in every culture, even if it doesn't rise to the physical destructiveness of the Taliban. The destructiveness at all levels of "either/or" thinking is hard to overemphasize, but it is particularly damaging to the development and use of curiosity, and consequently, to the development of the individual. Curiosity is the driving force behind learning, progress, and change. When we limit curiosity, we limit the expression of life itself.

Recall that interest is the driving force behind concentration. If we are not interested in what we are doing, or what is happening around us, we don't pay attention. If we don't pay attention, we don't learn. On the other hand, the more interested we are, the more curious we become, the greater our capacity to focus on the subject. The warrior sage cultivates curiosity about all aspects and elements of life. She realizes that the stronger her curiosity, the more effortless her discipline becomes.

As the warrior sage becomes more aware of subtle realities, she realizes that any answer is only a temporary shelter, a resting place from which to formulate a more penetrating, interesting question. Answers are never, and can never be, final about anything. The only constant in the material world is change, so any answer that we find is bound to reach a point where it is no longer relevant to the search or to the reality it once served. We expand awareness of the journey by asking better questions, not ever by finding an answer. The difficulty for most is that they hold on to answers even when those answers no longer serve them. This happens on a personal level, on an institutional level such as in religion and corporations, and on a social and cultural level. The more we cling to an answer, the more fixed in non-reality we become, and the greater our fear.

Curiosity is the mainsail of our journey, and we sail on the winds of change. It moves us into unknown realms with ease and excitement. Watch any child and you will see that child come alive under the power of curiosity. The same is true for all of us. The more we allow our curiosity to take us into the unknown, the greater our excitement, the more alive we feel, and the deeper we engage life. Name and fame, wealth, and power are driving forces for those dominated by the ego-self. But for the warrior sage, curiosity is the moving force that compels the journey and opens the most subtle of realities.

Curiosity is the driving force, but life itself provides the lessons and the opportunities. Life is the expression of the divine, and the warrior sage recognizes that in every instant, regardless of what is happening, there is an opportunity to experience the intelligence, power, and creative joy of the Divine. The increasing skill of the warrior sage allows her to use the intensity of any experience to become even more aware of the underlying realities. The more intense the experience, the greater is the opportunity to reach back into the source. Whether we arbitrarily characterize or judge the experience as good or bad, pain or pleasure, success or failure, each experience is an opportunity to become more aware, to grow as an individual, and to touch the infinite. By being attentive to the subtle nuances of life, the warrior sage is guided by life's journey.

Throughout the journey we are offered endless possibilities to create the life we want. Whether we choose to consciously participate or not, life is a process of spiritual expansion or awakening. This awakening is characterized by five evolutionary stages. In each stage, there is a core process that we must acquire as a skill that is essential to spiritual unfoldment. If we gain and retain skill in the process, we continue to grow throughout life. This process occurs so naturally in each stage that we tend to focus on the outcome of learning, and pay little attention to the process itself. But every outcome of learning, every answer, is fixed to the time and level in which we found it. The problem is that answers are like containers, and they limit awareness. It is not really the answers we find, but the process that is crucial to the expansion of awareness and development. In other words, we fall in love with the label and forget to retain the process. The warrior sage, on the other hand, systematically develops and expands the process, and practices non-attachment to the answers.

These five stages of process, beginning at birth, are interpenetrating and universal. These are not fixed in time, nor do they constitute a rigid classification. These are truly developmental, and expand and contract within each of us throughout life. Each human being, regardless of culture, race, belief or period, moves through these stages. And all five of these core processes are necessary to fulfill our human/spiritual destiny. These five stages are: the explorer, the scientist, the warrior, the dancer and the magician. The names of the stages are intended to reflect the internal process which is crucial to spiritual development.

The Explorer: The Foundation of Play

We begin life as an explorer. Although we may not look the part, and we spend the first few months eating and sleeping, the task we face immediately is to learn about the world around us and to explore who and what we are. Curiosity drives us, and we engage the world with a burning desire to discover the reality in which we find ourselves. In this stage, we must establish the foundation of our personality, the platform from which we operate for the rest of our life. This critical task, one of the most important that we ever face, determines in great part how we

live the rest of our life. In the first five to seven years of life, the ego-self
is formed. Learning is most intense, and the largest numbers of neurological networks are formed. Exploration is critical in this stage.

But how does an infant or small child explore? We do so through
the powerful process of play. Play is the first real lesson of life. The
process of play creates the crucial foundation upon which we build an
entire life. For the child, play is spontaneous, undefined, and unregu-
lated. Anything and everything is included in the playground. There
are no limits for the child to his curiosity and his willingness to engage.
Through play, the child experiences the delight of discovery. In Vedic
philosophy, the sages describe the manifest world as Lila, which means
cosmic or divine play, reflecting the unlimited creative spontaneity that
characterizes play.

Ideally, the child grows in an environment of love, security, and
the freedom to explore without punishment. When this does happen,
the ego-self grows without damage. The individual remains open-
minded, and becomes capable of giving and receiving. His curiosity
is nurtured, and he remains a life-long learner, fully willing to take the
risks and make the mistakes that are so necessary for learning to occur.

All too often, however, parents and society collaborate to "mold"
the personality into acceptable forms. The child is taught that only if he
acts in "socially acceptable ways" will he get the love and support necessary to grow. Play becomes sanctioned, rules are imposed, competition
is introduced, and winning the prize is the only acceptable outcome.
This means, of course, that failure becomes a significant demon. The
child is told to "draw inside the lines," to follow the rules, to behave
properly. Instead of being guided, the child is directed and formed,
becomes a good little boy or girl, and learns to fit the mold. After all,
adults know what this child should be! Nothing damages curiosity more
than being given and having to memorize all the right answers. Like
curiosity, sadly, by age seven we retain only a very small percentage of
our innate curiosity.

Fortunately, we can always relearn that crucial lesson, and again
learn how to play. In play, we stop worrying about results, and focus on
the delight of discovery. We stop trying to play by the rules, to do things

the right way, and simply enter into exploration and dance. When we use stillness as a way to gain insight, or we use an imagery exercise to go inside and have a conference with our imaginary advisors, it is an opportunity to play. To enter and utilize the creative matrix of the mind requires a playful attitude and an open, receptive mind, not one that is striving, full of rules and expectations, and working hard for an answer. The more striving we are, the more rules we impose, the further away from the natural creative force of the mind we find ourselves.

This is what practice is all about. Developing the power of the warrior sage is not about following the rules; it is about relearning how to play. Throughout the book we use the term practice. If we want to develop a skill, we must practice the appropriate behaviors. Because we have given up play, our concept of practice is an onerous one, something we must make ourselves do. For example, practicing meditation is far too serious for many. They work hard at becoming enlightened. After years of "hard work," they are often disappointed because it didn't produce what they expected. Really dedicated students push on, continuing to struggle while hoping for the best. The mistake being made is not meditation itself, but in how they approach their meditation. They see it as some task they must do to achieve their objective. In this way, it becomes work, and often onerous, boring work. This kind of practice never leads to enlightenment.

Practicing meditation is not an onerous task; it is an opportunity to dance with the mind. Using a mantra in meditation is not something we must do in order to achieve enlightenment or peace of mind, or whatever we do meditation for; it is a dancing partner to play in the field of mind and consciousness. The same is true of all practices done by the warrior sage. We engage a meditation practice, or any exercise, with attentive curiosity to see what unfolds for us in the moment. There is nowhere to go, and nothing to do, but there is a great deal to attend to, and in the attending, we expand our awareness and grow.

The very first demand of genuine self-discipline is knowing how to play. Most adults have forgotten this first lesson in life. But, for the warrior sage, play forms the foundation of effort and this opens the door to the joy of life and the immutable bliss of the spiritual-Self.

Self-discipline is more than just play, it requires systematic play. This brings us into the second stage where we learn and refine the second fundamental lesson of life, the process of experimentation.

The Scientist and the Experiment: Learning the Hows and Whys

As we play and grow in our capacity for exploration and discovery, there comes a time when we must begin to organize our experiences and knowledge. Now our activities as an explorer must take on new dimensions, and we enter the stage of the scientist. As a scientist, we must begin to order and systematize our play and knowledge so that we gain deeper insight into the hows and whys of the reality around us. This is typically when formal education begins, but formal education is not the requisite element of this stage. Up to this point, our play has been based solely on our whims and interests at the moment. We simply did what seemed most interesting to us at the time, and we explored what was immediately available to us. But now, a new level of learning must take place as our primary role as an explorer morphs into the role of a scientist.

As a scientist, we still play and explore, but do so in a way that leads to a greater depth of understanding. Our play must become more systematic in order to penetrate the obvious and find the more hidden, deeper realities. This is the role of the scientist – to postulate, to theorize, to think clearly about experiences rather than just to have them, to uncover the hidden realities that govern the more superficial ones. This requires that we add to the process of play the second crucial process of systematic search. Now we must begin to experiment, to set up conditions that allow us to learn the hidden facts, the more subtle forms of knowledge.

A true scientist is forever in search of truth, not someone who claims to know the truth. The warrior sage must become a scientist in the true meaning of the term. This implies several key qualities:

1. An open-minded skepticism, which build beliefs based on direct experience, evidence, and experimentation rather than book knowledge or theory;

2. A willingness to explore alternatives and resist dogmatism;

3. A search for cause/effect relationships;

4. Attention to details while retaining the ability to see the whole and understand relationships;

5. Recognition of belief systems, theories and paradigms as tools rather than immutable facts;

6. A willingness to test personal belief systems, to push the envelope, to test the limits of knowledge;

7. Development of creativity and insight as well as clarity and discrimination; use of logic but recognition of its limits and a willingness to go beyond.

The key process for the scientist is the experiment, the willingness to set up conditions that allow him to penetrate into the hidden aspects of knowledge. This includes both formal and informal opportunities. For the warrior sage, life is a series of experiments. He constantly attends to cause/effect relationships without judging. Not only does he observe his own inner experiments, but watches and learns from the experiments of others. In an experiment, the focus is on both the process and the outcome. Mistakes are understood as part of the process, and outcomes are recognized as only temporary answers. If the results are not what we expected, it simply means that we revise our expectation, and/or we alter the process and have a new experiment. This experimental attitude helps mitigate against being ego-invested in the outcome, and allows us to remain flexible, non-dogmatic and open to new ways of thinking, being, and acting.

Every practice, whether it is one for the mind, body, or spirit, is seen as an experiment. For example, meditation practice is an experiment in internal observation. One enters a meditation practice with curiosity to observe what is happening, not with some pre-set belief about what should happen. In this way, the practice remains both intense and interesting without effort. Curiosity remains the driving force in experimentation, not expectation.

The perspective of the warrior sage towards education is, again, quite different from the formal education that most suffer through. Formal education typically provides answers rather than teaching students how to think for themselves. Modern western education, with its emphasis on career development, is a training ground to provide cogs to run the economic system. The term "education" however, derives from the Greek word "educare," meaning "to bring out from within." We tell children what to think and what to do, but we rarely give children the tools they need to think for themselves. Education fails, and we fail, when we don't teach our children to experiment, to discover for themselves. We fail when we provide answers based on "authority" without providing the reasoning skills to verify for themselves.

The failure of our educational system is seen in the great mass of individuals who are no longer curious about life. Instead, they turn to materialism, far more interested in obtaining material things than in personal growth and development. Even when personal growth is emphasized, it is almost always tied to "career development," and seen as a tool for even greater material gain. They often lose the spark of life, the excitement of discovery about the world and themselves that is the natural consequence of curiosity, play, and experimentation. They turn to alternative highs, such as drugs, extreme sports, even violence. Another disturbing example is the growing problem of teen-age suicide, an indication that the emptiness and futility of materialism, or the sense of failure and unacceptability, have become overwhelming.

For the warrior sage, self-mastery demands self-training, the systematic use of experimentation, study, and practice, guided by curiosity and characterized with self-discipline. As the architect of his own life, he takes full "response ability" for his own education. A teacher, master, guru, or tradition, will not provide the answer; only access to the means. The warrior sage utilizes the means and takes charge of his own educational development. As he refines his knowledge and skill, he moves into the third stage of life, testing himself, his knowledge, and his skills in the world around him.

The Warrior: Winning and Losing as Acts of Fearlessness

There comes a time when we must go out into the world and express the knowledge gained through exploration and experimentation. The warrior stage is a time to test our knowledge, strengths, and weaknesses. The warrior stage represents the expression of knowledge and skill, a conquest of elements and weaknesses. It is not the conquest of others, but of one's own nature that determines the achievement of the warrior. It is a time of reaching out, into, and to the world, a time of testing, and a time of a gain and loss, or as some would say, of winning and losing, success and failure. Our life now centers on the work we engage and the independent life we create for ourselves. We can no longer rely on our parents and our teachers. It is up to us to make that life satisfying, to create a sense of accomplishment, and to realize that we truly are the architect of our life.

It is in this stage that we take responsibility for growing up and we contribute to the world around us. The warrior stage is not defined by profession, but involves everything we do. While the world of work is the central arena in the warrior stage, it is not the only one. To fulfill the stage of the warrior, we must become a complete person and integrate all facets of life. A warrior must maximize versatility even though he or she becomes a specialist in a chosen profession. For the warrior sage, success in this stage is not determined by a particular level of income, prestige, or power, but rather, by the expression of skill, the developing sense of accomplishment, and recognition of one's abilities, whether it is brain surgery, dairy farming, full-time mother, or hotel clerk.

In the warrior stage, the crucial lesson is to overcome fear and act fearlessly as we win and lose on the world stage. As we gain greater skill in directing the power of the mind, we quickly learn that fear is nothing more than a habit of the mind. Fear is not an innate quality of the human being. No human child is born with fear. We learn to be fearful, and that impacts and limits everything we do. As long as we continue to create the habit of fear for ourselves, we can never escape the clutches and limits of the ego-self. The journey of the warrior sage is, in many ways, a journey into fearlessness. This lesson is not complete until we transcend the ego-self through the spiritual disciplines. Typically, it is in the warrior stage that this transcendence first occurs, and then finds completion in the final two stages of life.

The first benefit of becoming fearless is the freedom to explore beyond the artificial limits set by culture, beliefs, and habits. When we thoughtlessly embrace cultural limitations and expectations, we become fearful of the judgments of others. Only by going beyond the fear of what others think do we begin to free ourselves from our own limitations and judgments. This allows us to make mistakes, try new ways of thinking and being in the world, and open our creative force. We now engage adversity with humor, joy, and a wonderful sense of challenge instead of fear, stress, and apprehension. This, in turn, opens up even greater opportunities for self-expression and growth.

Only by acting fearlessly do we learn that winning and losing are only arbitrary designations. Within the divine, nothing is ever lost or gained. Of course, everything changes, and change is the source of what we call gain and loss. But the attitude we have about change indicates the degree of our attachment to having life be a certain way in order for us to be secure, content, and happy. This kind of security, contentment and happiness actually breeds insecurity because the only constant is change. At the deepest levels of the mind we know that change is inevitable. When we seek gain and try to avoid loss, and base our happiness, security, and well-being on material possessions, we resist change and create a foundation of fear. This limits both personal growth and spiritual-Self realization, and we grow increasingly more fearful and more limited in thought, action, and expression. If we truly are the on-board representative of the divine, then there is no such thing as winning or losing.

Becoming fearless and recognizing that gain or loss is nothing more than arbitrary illusion opens the unlimited potential that exists within. This crucial shift often dramatically occurs with the first experience of transcendence, the moment when we first experience the spiritual-Self. Up to this point, the journey is predominantly one of transformation as we move from being fearful, striving, self-absorbed, and conflicted to an individual who is fearless, skilled in using the resources of the mind and body, lives with integrity, and is motivated by curiosity. This is self-mastery, and the spiritual discipline of prayer plays a key role. But the dawning of spiritual-Self realization through meditation shifts the intention of the warrior sage. We become more joyful in our play and experimentation, and we enter into the fourth stage of life. Now transcendence takes center stage as we begin to shift identity from the ego-self to the core of our being, the spiritual-Self. This does not mean that the transformation is complete. There is no end-point, no final goal to learning and development. For the warrior sage, life is process, not a series of goals to achieve and claim. And in process, what counts is how we play the game.

The Dancer: Freedom, Action and Self-Expression

As we refine the resources of the body/mind complex through play, experiment, and fearlessness, and experience the reality of the spiritual-Self through spiritual discipline, the warrior sage embraces the joyful reality of life and enters the stage of the dancer. For the dancer, winning and losing are totally irrelevant; success and failure are one and the same. Now is the time for refinement – of skill, of insight, of self-expression. Actions are taken not for accomplishment, but because they are in harmony with "what is." There is no sense of striving, no punishing need to accomplish, and no demanding expectation to fulfill. There is only the ever-enlarging opportunity to dance, to express oneself in the clearest, most harmonious fashion.

The crucial lesson of the fourth stage is to learn to dance, to express oneself free of any compulsion, directed only by the opportunity for full expression. There is nothing to do, nowhere to go, nothing to achieve – there is only the dance. For the warrior sage, the focus is on the subtle aspects of body, mind, and spirit, a discovery of new ways of being and acting in the world. It is here that the spiritual-Self comes to the fore, and we use the body/mind complex as a tool for expression. This is a time of mentorship to others, of teaching, of giving back to the community at large. We are no longer concerned with building a separate life – developing careers, establishing reputation, or creating wealth. For the dancer, the focus is self-expression without the need for reward, and for giving back – to ourselves, to our families, and to our communities. It is a time when we begin to live in the spirit instead of for the spirit.

There is a story told by Joseph Campbell about the time he took a number of American businessmen on a trip to Japan. They visited a number of Japanese temples and shrines, and after several visits, one of the businessmen engaged a Shinto priest in a conversation. "I have visited several Shinto temples," he said, "but I don't understand your theology; I don't understand your ideology."

The priest was quiet for a moment, and then responded, "We don't have a theology, we don't have an ideology. We dance."

This is the freedom of the dancer – unrestricted by dogma or ideology, not limited by belief or theology, the dancer simply moves within the spirit, acting sometimes wisely, sometimes foolishly, but always in harmony with the dance. There is no form to follow, no role to be; for the dancer there is only the dance. For the warrior sage, everything is part of the dance – happiness or sorrow, wealth or poverty, success or failure – all the polarities are engaged, all the contradictions are embraced, and all the limits are abolished. In this process of refinement, he experiences the sacred triangle of knowledge, will and action in the material reality as well as in the spiritual reality. It is a time of genuine freedom and growing power.

In the refinement of the dance, the warrior sage transcends the ego-self and experiences the fullness of the spiritual-Self. In this continuing re-cognition of divinity, he moves through the portal of the spiritual-Self, and enters the final stage, the endless, eternal stage of the magician.

The Magician: Self, Identity and Divinity

This, the final lesson, entails the movement through the portal of the spiritual-Self and realizing the fullness of divinity. The magician represents both the transcendental experience and the power of manifestation. In this stage, which begins in time but reaches into infinity, the warrior sage experiences both the transcendent and immanent power of God. The final lesson, if we can even speak of this as a lesson, is to step into the mystery of the divine, and recognize that "All This Am I." In the tantric tradition, this is referred to as the supreme experience, and signifies the fulfillment of the journey. There is little to describe in this stage because it is beyond all description. There are no tasks to accomplish, no lessons to learn, only the re-cognition of divinity.

This will seem strange to the mind limited by belief and dogma, but for the warrior sage, it is the culmination of direct experience. Belief is unnecessary for the attainment of the magician, just as belief is unnecessary for the journey of the warrior sage. The only thing that counts is the knowledge gained through direct experience. Spiritual traditions are spiritual traditions because they lead to direct spiritual experience, not because of the beliefs or philosophies they use to define Reality or God.

The words and descriptions written in this book are only words and descriptions. The Reality is quite different. The truth of the divine is not an analytic truth, it is not a concept, and it is not a belief. It is only found in direct experience. It is the purpose, and the fulfillment of the warrior sage to take that journey, to refine awareness, to move through the stages of life, and to take our place within the Ancient One.

Chapter Nine
Transcendence – Realizing the Ancient One

*The most ancient traveler in the world is love,
which travels from eternity to eternity.*
—His Holiness Swami Rama—

Transcendence is the experiential shift in identity from the ego-self to the spiritual-Self and ultimately, through the spiritual discipline of contemplation, to the Universal Self. It is *recognition*, or *re-cognition*, of the most fundamental truth of our being: that we truly are nothing less than divinity itself. It is not becoming something different, but rather awakening to the most subtle resources of power, intelligence, and joy. There is no place to go, nothing to achieve, and no one to become. It is not a matter of change, but a growing awareness of who we already are.

Transcendence is most often a gradual process of letting go of old identities and accessing this spiritual power that lies within. For a very few, transcendence can be a jolting flash, catapulting the individual into a radical change of meaning and value – Saint Paul for instance. Saint Paul was originally named Saul and was a Jewish fundamentalist who delighted in persecuting and killing early Christians. On a trip to Damascus to continue his persecution, Saul was struck blind by a great light, and remained blind for three days. In that time, his entire inner being was transformed, and he became a devout Christian whose thoughts and beliefs have become a dominant force in modern Christianity. But for most, it is a slow, gentle awakening that gradually reshapes the interior world, a consequence of the challenging process of developing skills and expanding awareness. There are no "7 easy steps" to enlightenment, but there are traditions, disciplines, and practices that lead us to our goal. Our first experience of transcendence or enlightenment, the conscious awareness of the spiritual-Self, is just the beginning of the journey, not the end. Often the first intense mystical experience is like being taken to the top of the mountain and shown the entire view. We don't stay there because we don't have the *adhikara* (the competence) to maintain this state of wakefulness. To establish lasting residence within the spiritual-Self, we must refine our skills within the spiritual disciplines. As we become more skilled, we expand into the endless space of Universal Consciousness. This process of expansion is one that never ends because the creative will of the divine is endless.

Just as each spiritual journey is unique, with underlying fundamental principles, so to is the character of each warrior sage. We are each unique in our personality, and this doesn't change as we grow into a warrior sage. The ego-self doesn't disappear; it becomes a mirror for the spiritual-Self, polished by the grinding stone of self-discipline and burnished by spiritual fire. As skill and awareness expands, our identity shifts from the ego-self to the spiritual-Self, eventually culminating in complete recognition of the divinity within. Spiritual-Self realization changes the way we experience life and material reality. Being a warrior sage does not make us a perfect person – we still make mistakes, we don't have all the answers, and we still feel sorrow and pain. But we do become an accomplished human being, skilled in the physical, mental, and spiritual disciplines that lead to transcendence, and who exhibits the wisdom, joy, freedom, and spontaneity that characterize the sage.

Don't confuse the warrior sage for the stereotype of a "holy person," the kind of individual who struggles to be nice, predictable, safe to be around, and talks about "holy things" all the time. We often see this in people who decide to be spiritual, and make sure that everyone knows about it. They often wear distinctive clothing or accessories, talk about giving themselves to God, not withstanding that none of them ever ask God's opinion about this. They often bless you and make sure that you know they are doing "the Lord's work" (as if they had the capacity of the Lord to do so). They say all the things that a "holy person" is supposed to say, and are constantly telling you and others what God wants us to do, for they know the mind of God. It's written down in their holy book! This is not spirituality; this is the rigid expression of an ego trip arrogantly confusing belief with truth.

A warrior sage is unpredictable, and often dangerous to the established order. His only governing laws are those of inner harmony, compassion, and love. He is often viewed as a threat by narrow-minded religionists who live "under the law," invoking God's name for their own beliefs and limitations. The religionist will tell you about what God wants you to do, while the warrior sage will always ask "What do you, as divinity, choose?" The greater the spiritual accomplishment, the greater the freedom from conventional rigidity in thought and action, and the more spontaneous life becomes. For a warrior sage, the only restrictions are those that lead to increasing freedom and greater harmony.

Much of what is written about transcendence has an almost magical quality – experiencing oneself as light, of being timeless and eternal, of being totally free of bodily restrictions, and even hearing celestial music. There are wonderful, inspiring descriptions of enlightenment, and although some descriptions are pure imagination, much of what is written is quite real. As one would expect, there are great varieties of experiences and viewpoints which overlie the common thread of Universal Consciousness. But nearly all descriptions speak about the felt experience, and seldom do we hear about the practical aspects of enlightenment. For the warrior sage, letting go of identification with the ego-self brings access to powerful and practical resources that typically exist only as ideals for the ordinary individual.

Transcendence: Realizing the Power of Divinity

Spiritual-Self realization – transcendence – is the tipping point in human development. The shift out of ego-self identity is literally reality-changing in its impact on the individual and in its implications for the larger society. The history of mankind is littered with paradigms, laws, and religious beliefs. For thousands of years we have attempted to control our animal nature through law and religious instruction. Our history is the history of the ego-self. It is time for another history, one dominated by the spiritual-Self and swaraj, or self-control. This can only happen through transcendence from within, not through law, instruction, or religious evangelism.

No matter how healthy the ego-self becomes, it is a limited reality. The ego cannot escape from the conditioning limits of thought and action, nor the impact of external influences. The ego-self, organized by its habits and patterns, and driven by the primitive urges of self-preservation, food, sleep, and sex, is enslaved by its own organization. The ego-self always, and necessarily, thinks in terms of "I, me, myself, and mine." Recall from an earlier discussion that the basic function of the ego is to form a limited center of identity. This allows the ego to organize and manage the various functions of the mind and body complex. But the more ego-self centered we become, the more limited we become until we are firmly bound in an increasingly smaller world in order to feel some kind of happiness and security.

Transcendence shifts our sense of personal identity from the ego-self to the unlimited spiritual-Self, and we experience a growing freedom from these inner driving forces that comprise and dominate the ego-self. Spiritual traditions recognize that the real struggle is the battle to overcome these inner dragons, the driving forces of the ego-self. External forces only seem powerful because we face them from the limited strength, wisdom, and capability of the ego-self. As we transcend this limited ego-self and function more clearly from the spiritual-Self, external forces no longer have the power to affect us in the same dramatic ways.

We need spiritual disciplines to engage this battle with the inner dragons. As we shift identity, and become more and more established within the spiritual-Self, we become more and more selfless. The attachments that are so important to the ego-self to enhance and protect itself become less necessary and important. Of course, the more skilled we become, the greater is the shift, until identity with the spiritual-Self is complete and we are no longer enslaved by our attachment to the ego-self.

When we become universal, there are no limitations. There is no little "I" to be concerned with. We all experience this shift in small ways throughout life, but we typically remain unaware of the hidden power in this experience. Recall the time when you were so focused on a task that you forgot about time. There was no sense of "me" or "mine" at that time. Or recall the time when you were shopping, and found "the perfect gift" for a loved one. Again, there was no sense of "I, me, or mine" as you imagined the look of delight and happiness on your loved one's face. Or recall the time you watched your child being born. For most, this is a time of great joy, a high point in life that we retain in our memory for a long time. In these moments, we become selfless and experience the power of bliss and the absence of any constraints or limitations that characterize the little ego-self. We don't disappear; we become fully present to the moment. These brief moments of selflessness increasingly become our daily reality as we shift personal identity to the spiritual-Self.

Selflessness, Love, and the Ancient One

We experience this selflessness, this disappearance of the limitations of the ego-self, as bliss. Bliss is one of the three words used in yoga philosophy and science to describe the indefinable God-head. These three words are existence (*sat*), consciousness (*chit*) and bliss (*ananda*). In more Western terms, we may translate this as God is everywhere (omnipresent), God is awareness, creative intelligence and power (omniscient, omnificent and omnipotent), and God is love. As we transcend the ego-self and shift identity to the spiritual-Self we experience this love, power and deathlessness. This is the power and true benefit of transcendence.

We are not describing the personality, which is a construction of the ego-self and nothing more than a tool for our use. Remember, for a warrior sage, the body/mind complex, organized by the ego-self and structured as a personality, is nothing more than a tool. Our true Self, the spiritual-Self, the soul or on-board representative of the divine, is the portal by which we enter into divinity or the Godhead itself. The spiritual-Self is the repository of the power, not the personality. The personality is the tool we use to express the power of God just as you would use a hammer to drive a nail. There are powerful people, but this power is limited until the ego-self is transcended, and the full power of the divine is made available.

Transcendence is an organic, synergistic process. Recall that it is the ego-self that has goals and achievements. For the spiritual-Self there is only the dance of Self-expression. Love, the experience of self-lessness, signals the end of the ego-self as the driving force. In this way, love is the entry into the full power of the divine. Love, my spiritual master Swami Rama was fond of saying, "is the most ancient traveler in the universe." The more selfless we are, the more loving we become, and the more power we experience as a human being. Love – not frailty, not hatred, not sin – is the very core of our humanity. Recall Plato's assertion that the core of humanity is divinity, or the ancient Hebrew injunction to love thy neighbor as thyself. Through transcendence, we consciously experience being the love that we already are.

Love is characterized by selflessness. This is not the love of love songs and poetry, which really celebrate emotional attachment. When most people speak of love they are really talking about emotional attachment. But even here, there still exists that ever-present kernel of genuine love that is the true source of the beauty, truth, and acceptance we feel when we are "in love." In emotional attachment, our ego-self is busy trying to establish a proprietary relationship with the person or object that it mistakenly thinks is the source of these wonderful feelings. We think we need the love of others because we are unaware of the love that we are. And when we gain the love of others, it does not fulfill our longing, nor does it end our loneliness. The love of others is wonderful, but the real benefit – that which brings us bliss, joy, and fulfillment and the end of loneliness – comes from consciously being the love that we already are. The warrior sage does not say "I love you" but rather "I am love with you."

Genuine love is a disappearing act of the ego-self. We experience the bliss of the divine, when the sense of "I, me, or mine" disappears, and we become unlimited and universal. At that moment we are free of attachments, of fears and concerns, of desires and wants. This passing moment becomes more sustained the more we practice being selfless. Being selfless does not mean that you become "all things to all people" and give away everything you have. Here the term "selfless" means being free from our fears, desires, and attachments and being able to choose rather than react out of habit. We become selfless to the degree that we are skilled at non-attachment and no longer identify with the limited ego-self. We are fully present at that moment, established in the spiritual-Self. This love, this Ancient One, is the source of great strength, harmony, joy, and wisdom, the practical outcomes of transcendence.

As we become more skilled at being the love that we already are, the habits of fear and self-hatred that can dominate an ego-self, and lead to destructive thoughts and behaviors, no longer have the power to determine and limit what we do. Emotions, for instance, no longer direct the behavior, but are utilized for the information process that they really are. Emotions are indicators that our thoughts and actions, or the situations in which we find ourselves, are either in or out of the deep harmony that characterizes the spiritual dimension. Instead of being used by our emotions, we are able to use and direct this powerful resource to be more effective in what we do.

For example, there are situations where anger is the only appropriate response. When the ego-self dominates, we experience the anger as ourselves, and our thoughts and actions are dominated by the anger. In other words, the anger controls us, defining our thoughts and actions. We may be afraid to express our anger, or we may over-react and create even further problems. Consequently, our mind and body suffer the consequences, as well as whomever may be the beneficiary of that anger. Often we carry the anger from one situation to another, often looking for another fight, another place to express the emotional energy. Of course, this only leads to more difficult situations, and an expanding circle of bad feeling spreads from one situation to another and from one person to another.

For a warrior sage, anger indicates the existence of disharmony. Instead of identifying with the emotion of anger, he utilizes anger as a tool. When we don't identify with the anger, we maintain an inner calm and clarity and are not overwhelmed by the anger. In this way we respond creatively and effectively to the situation, using the anger in specific and targeted ways. By not identifying with the anger, we prevent the anger from generating stress hormones inside the body and damaging the heart or raising blood pressure. By directing the anger in appropriate ways and with the appropriate intensity, we are far more effective in utilizing the anger to correct the specific situation and not carry the anger from one situation to the next.

As awareness of the transcendental identity of the spiritual-Self expands, a warrior sage becomes more inner directed and less compelled not only by his own mental patterns (emotions, beliefs, habits) but also by arbitrary social forces and pressures. He no longer reacts to life, but rather responds from his own sense of harmony, wisdom, and compassion. We still experience emotions, make mistakes, and face the same obstacles that everyone else must face. However, we no longer have any need to define ourselves by what happens in the external world. We are present to, and in alignment with, the eternal presence of the divine.

Compassion: Love in Action

The unlimited power (Consciousness) of the divine is never separate from bliss, the unlimited love of the divine. So too in a warrior sage, power experienced on a personal level is never separate from the quality of love. This inseparable combination of power and love is the source of compassion, strength, and wisdom. When love interacts with the world it takes the form of compassion. This is the power of the human spirit which Gandhi referred to as *satyagraha*. Gandhi saw this force as a substitute for violence. In liberating love and compassion, the power of the human spirit, we have a power far stronger than hate and fear.

Compassion is a natural outcome of transcendence. Life means action and relationship, but the actions we take and the relationships we form are determined by whether we are ego-centered or spirit-centered. As transcendence shifts identity to the spiritual-Self, we become more compassionate and less sympathetic. We feel sympathy for others when we feel powerless to alter the circumstances that lead to pain. Compassion arises when we acknowledge suffering and we take actions to alleviate that suffering. The warrior sage, by recognizing that suffering is limited to the ego-self, returns to the source and directs his power with clarity and effectiveness to help relieve suffering.

All great spiritual traditions strive to eliminate suffering. They do so by going to the root of the problem: ignorance of our spiritual nature. The thrust is not to fix something, but to eliminate ignorance at all levels. Compassionate people build hospitals and schools, provide means for self-support, and develop resources to provide opportunities for growth and development. They respect the power that each individual has to eliminate suffering for themselves as long as they have the means. The question is never what to give, but how to develop the inner strength, power, and freedom of those that suffer. Sympathy often leads to actions that create dependency, but acts of compassion lead to independence and self-rule.

We are all compassionate when we become free from the demands and needs of the limited ego-self. Compassion can never be forced, but neither can it be denied when transcendence occurs. Love is a force that moves outward from the center of our being, and not something that takes for itself. The more we practice selflessness and the more loving we become, the more our actions arise from the spiritual-Self and the more compassionate we become. It is the natural expression of love in action. In this expression, there is enormous strength.

Inner Strength and Gentleness

Recall from Chapter 6 that the spiritual discipline of meditation leads to inner strength and a powerful will. This provides a warrior sage with genuine self-confidence that is free of any self-doubts. For those locked into the ego-self, will is a struggle for domination, and confidence is based on winning and success. Fear of losing often makes this strength rigid, and can eventually lead to violence in one form or another. But love and compassion tempers the expression of unlimited inner strength, creating flexibility as well as determination. We can be unmovable when necessary, but also move with ease through the changing realities we all face.

The defining characteristic of genuine inner strength is gentleness. Genuinely strong individuals are not rough and tough, even when they are intense and determined. The love, attention, and guidance of my spiritual master were like a diamond – brilliant in its compassion and concern, but hard and unyielding in its demand for my own growth. His anger was never abusive, but there was no escape from his wrath. It was always cleansing and purifying, and he never left me afraid or wounded. The pain he was able to create for me was always precise and pointed, excising the ego-driven issue that was the point of the anger, but never damaging the surrounding tissue of my spirit.

We all have this inner resource of strength and self-confidence, but when filtered through the ego-self, it often becomes demanding, hard, and inflexible. It serves the habits and patterns of the ego-self, and is often buried beneath the weight of fear and worry. The ego-self, unaware of the source of inner strength, builds confidence by being successful. As long as we are successful, we feel very confident. But success is not a constant of life, and so we build this confidence on a shifting bed of sand. When we aren't successful, when everything goes wrong, we lose confidence, and must struggle to find it again.

Genuine self-confidence is built on inner strength that lies within the very core of our being, the spiritual-Self. It is already a part of who we are, and we have all experienced it at some time or the other. Recall a time when you were taking a walk by yourself. It may have been in a park, on the beach, or even just around the neighborhood. All of a sudden, you felt like "God was in the heavens, and all was right with the world." For a few moments, you experienced a freedom from all your needs, fears, and wants. There was no struggle with anything or anyone, and no need to dominate or win. Instead, you felt contentment, fullness, and completeness. It may have lasted only a few moments, but you came back from your walk ready to take on the world again. You didn't take drugs, you didn't win a fortune, and you didn't change jobs.

What you did was simply let go of the patterns and habits of the ego-self for a few brief moments, and experienced a touch of the spiritual-Self. What if, in the middle of the day when all the alligators were biting at your heels and you were struggling with problems and concerns, you could drop your gaze for a moment, focus on your breath, and experience this incredible feeling that you had on the walk? What would happen to your self-confidence?

Through transcendence, this "brief moment" of strength becomes a constant companion. When this happens, there is no need to push, no striving to achieve, and no fear of loss. Instead, you feel a quiet strength that has no need to struggle, dominate, or resist. You experience gentleness, a softness or yielding that is free of any threat or insecurity. But don't be misled. This gentleness of genuine inner strength is neither weak nor ineffectual. It is irresistible, like water coming down a mountain. It is soft and yielding when necessary, moving and powerful when appropriate. As the consequence of transcendence and a resource of the spiritual-Self, this inner strength is free of weaknesses of the ego-self.

This inner strength is already inside each and every one of us, and a warrior sage builds a pathway to this resource through the spiritual disciplines. This experience is called by various names – yoga (union), Christ-consciousness; enlightenment, walking in the Tao – indicating that fusion of personal identity with the spiritual-Self. With this inner strength, we are completely fearless, able to love freely, and to act compassionately. All of this allows us to walk with wisdom, making choices out of our creative intelligence.

Wisdom: Opening to Creative Intelligence

One of the most practical outcomes of transcendence is the direct access to the creative intelligence (omnificence) of the divine which provides increasing clarity and wisdom. We often think that wisdom is a function of age and experience, and to some degree it is. Both age and experience allow us to step away from our ego to some degree, and gain a greater perspective about life. Our wisdom depends greatly on the degree to which we reflect upon our experiences and learn from them.

But the wisdom we gain is indirect and limited as long as we remain identified with the ego-self. We mistakenly think that wisdom is a function of how smart we are, how great an intellect we are; but in truth, wisdom is quite different.

A warrior sage recognizes that the source of wisdom is not the mind, but rather arises out of the creative intelligence (omnificence) of the divine. Divinity is the fundamental ground of all being, and all reality resides within God. Creative intelligence is an aspect of Consciousness. Just as Newton didn't create gravity, we don't create truth. We become more deeply aware or conscious of a reality that already exists within the divine. This awareness we call knowledge. How we interpret or make sense of that reality is a function of the intellect. The intellect is a function of the mind, a processing tool by which mind creates categories, names, and forms, the stuff of knowledge. Intellect is our ability to make connections about and within material reality. Intelligence is the pure knowledge itself.

In *Evolutions End*, Joseph Chilton Pearce points out that intellect asks, "Can it be done?" while intelligence asks "Should it be done?" When ego-self dominates, then intellect rules, but this rule is subject to the weaknesses of the ego-self. Under any perceived threat, the powerful intellect is used for ego-self preservation, and we build powerful weapons of mass destruction. In other words, the intellect, as a tool of the ego-self, will serve whatever fear, greed, or other emotion dominates the ego-self.

Creative intelligence is still the foundation, but remains buried beneath the emotional demands of the ego. If we reflect on our experiences, we are capable of going beyond the habits, needs and fears of the ego-self to some degree, and gaining some degree of wisdom. But for most, identified with the ego-self, wisdom is haphazard and difficult to come by.

Through transcendence, a warrior sage escapes the limitations that bind the ego-self, and consciously enters the infinite field of creative knowledge. We think more clearly and penetrate more deeply into the nature of the reality which surrounds us. No longer limited by the emotional habits that color and distort the perceptions of the ego-self, we see things as they are. Our power of discrimination becomes more and more refined, discerning greater degrees of harmony as we penetrate into the deeper nature of things. Our choices now reflect this increased awareness of reality and harmony, allowing us to act wisely and effectively in the world.

We now understand wisdom as the ability to act in accordance with a deeper harmony of truth/reality than most people are able to know and achieve. Wisdom doesn't depend on how smart we are. There are a great many very smart people with great intellects who act with very little wisdom. Unfortunately, because they are very smart, they often become powerful and influential leaders. The inevitable outcomes are the human disasters that characterize the world today. Intellect without wisdom is a path to destruction. Transcendence is the only practical answer to this problem. The entry into creative intelligence provides not only the wisdom we need to solve the problems we face, but it also provides us with the creativity necessary to find new ways of solving problems and meeting challenges.

Creativity and Change

The reality of change provides a constant opportunity for creativity. Awareness of both the ego-self and the spiritual-Self provide a warrior sage with the opportunity to respond to changing realities with insight, innovation, and effectiveness. Again, transcendence allows creativity full play because we are no longer limited by the habitual patterns of thought and reaction that characterize the ego-self. We are free to respond rather than react, and with deeper insight and greater access to the power of discrimination, we have an increasingly unlimited playing field. And play is a key element in the creative process. As a dancer, a warrior sage is free of the self-doubts, the striving, and the fear of mistakes that so often inhibit the creative response.

Reality is the play of divine creative intelligence. This creative intelligence is echoed in the human mind, which itself is a creative process. Everyday we create the reality of meaning which defines our personal world. This process, however, of meaning-making is shaped and constrained by the mental function of habituation. Habituation is a necessary and powerful force in the human mind. It impacts all aspects of the human experience – how and what we think, the words we use, and, of course, our behavior. It creates consistency, conserves both energy and effort, and allows us to function in the world with ease. When we take conscious control of this powerful mental process, we build skills and become disciplined. Left unexamined and undirected, this powerful tool leads to unconscious but powerful constraints and limitations. The crucial point is that habits are only powerful as long as they remain in the unconscious mind.

The creative play of the divine, however, is unlimited and unrestrained. Transcendence, the experiential shift from identifying with the ego-self to the spiritual Self, allows a warrior sage to enter the unlimited creative play of the divine. As we become established in the spiritual-Self, and expand awareness into Universal Consciousness, we move from the stage of the dancer into that of the magician. We now begin to experience and engage the full power of the creative intelligence of the divine. In alignment with sat, chit, ananada – with the eternal existence, consciousness and bliss of the divine – we achieve the final freedom from the bondage of even the most subtle of attachments. This is the ultimate goal, called *moksa* in the tantric tradition, and referred to as "sitting on the right hand of God" in the Christian tradition. We, as a warrior sage, live in complete harmony with the divine.

Harmony and the Moral Self

The laws and principles of all spiritual and religious traditions are the reflection of a great truth that is seldom understood. In the heart of our humanity lies divinity, the source of all morality. At this level, moral relevancy does not exist because time, culture, or beliefs do not exist. As a warrior sage, ethics and morality are who we are, and all the rules, laws, and commandments are irrelevant to the living truth of this inner divinity. As a warrior sage, we live in harmony with ourselves and others, with our surroundings, and with nature. As we become aware of this inner source, as we evolve into a warrior sage, our actions, thoughts and speech arise from this moral source, and we no longer "follow the rules." Instead, we live the principles. We are not violent because there is no violence inside us. We are strong, powerful, and even forceful when appropriate, but violence is not force or strength. Violence is the overuse of force because of emotional energy generated by fear, hatred, greed, or lust. It is a clear and certain sign of weakness.

There is a natural ethic, a natural order that is inherent in all humanity. It does not arise from the ego-self at all, it is not decided by any philosophy or theology or political system; it is divinity itself. This natural ethic is power – the power of joy, the power of intelligence, the power of awareness. As said above, there is no hate in divinity, there is no violence in divinity – there is only God. As a warrior sage, identified with divinity, we experience the deep harmony of this natural ethic, and it is this natural ethic that guides our behavior. We are free from the tyranny of law and belief, and fully engaged ethically.

This is what Gandhi ultimately meant by *swaraj*. When we experience the deep harmony of divinity as our Self, we have no need to harm others, to take advantage, or to grasp wealth, power, or fame to feel competent, secure, or important. There is no need to live by the "laws of God" when we are the Divinity Itself. Strict "believers" and those who only see humanity as inherently evil may rail against this statement, but this anger is driven by a need to control, not by spiritual experience and insight. Egocentric beliefs, shaped by emotions, and often unexamined and unchallenged, lock them into unreflective slavery, and prevent them from experiencing the harmony of spiritual union.

By living our divinity, we actually become the change we want to see in others. We are not ethical or moral simply because we follow the law or embrace a religion; we are moral because our inner nature is the natural ethic of divinity. Until we experience this infinite and perfect divinity as our own Self, we are only partly human, and partly human beings controlled by weak ego-selves can be fearful, hateful, and dangerous.

Sin: Original and Otherwise

All great religious and spiritual traditions provide ethical and moral principles that are meant to guide behavior. These basic principles of all religions and spiritual traditions, and their intent, are very

similar – how to live in ways which contribute to personal welfare and
to the greater welfare of all. Along with these principles are rules and
laws in which the only purpose is to sustain the structure and rule of
the authorities of the particular religion. We find the same in the larger
societies in which religions exist. All societies have rules and laws, from
the most primitive tribal customs to sophisticated tomes of legalisms, all
designed to protect members of the tribe or society, and/or to sustain
the structure and protect the rulers of the same.

The difficulty does not lie in the intent of the moral principles, but
rather in the unthinking, slavish obedience to these principles, as well as
to the rules and laws often demanded by religious and civil authorities,
and most often, by our own embedded belief systems. Often expressed
as "God's Law," they are presented by religious authorities as dictums
as to what "God wants us to do." Religious authority always claims it
knows the mind of God, and going against the law means that we have
sinned against God. Religions offer a variety of protocols whereby one
can repent of his sins and be saved from hellfire and eternal damna-
tion. Of course, we are supposedly free to choose, but you better make
the choice that the authorities have decided for you. "Good" Catholics
do what the Catholic Church tells them to do, "good" Protestants do
what the preacher tells them to do, "good" Jews follow the letter of the
law, "good" Muslims do what the mullahs tell them to do, and "good"
citizens do what the government tells them to do. The greatest danger
is the confluence of religious belief and civil government. Fundamentalists of all religions struggle to make their particular religious beliefs
the law of the greater society, hoping to achieve "one great ant hill" of
conformity to their beliefs.

There exists a chronic tension between freedom of choice and
the rules and laws of religion and society. Philosophers and theologians
valiantly struggle with the inherent conflicts that arise between choice
and law, attempting to reach the balance necessary between control
and choice. Serious thought recognizes that this rarely comes down to
an either/or situation, a matter of black and white, but mostly involves
choices between two goods or the lesser of two evils. In other words,
there is a lot of gray in the area of ethics, morality, and law. While

this great debate will necessarily continue as long as we are ruled by the ego-self, a simple fact remains: rules and laws are made by weak people to protect themselves from other weak people who have more power, but lack inner strength. You don't have to protect yourself from someone who operates from the love, strength, and harmony of the spiritual-Self.

The entire history of mankind is a record of abuse, particularly from those who are more powerful towards those less powerful. History shows clearly that every society must protect itself from those who are willing to harm others, whether in the name of religion, manifest destiny, economic development (often nothing more than a cover name for pure greed), hatred, or political necessity. Unfortunately, the practice of religion has had little impact on this history. In fact, as said earlier, religions, and particularly evangelistic fundamentalists of all religions, are often the source of conflict, wars, terrorism, and domination. The truth is that religious conflict, empiricism, and cultural domination have been constants in human history. We still wage holy wars, we still claim to have God on our side, we still struggle to have more than the next fellow, and we still have police, armies, and rulers.

This will not change as long as ego-selves rule. Those who claim to know God and act to harm others do not know divinity at all, only their own ego needs and fears. The God of every religion is made in the religion's own image of man, which is controlled and instructed by ego-selves. For the ego-self, there are differences to be argued and defended, fears and desires to be acted upon, and enemies and evil to combat. Hatred, intolerance, violence, evil – all belong to the world of the ego-self. Those ruled by the ego-self suffer these within themselves, and then project them into the world.

There is no hatred in God, there is no intolerance in God, there is no evil in God, and there is no sin in God. For the warrior sage who lives inside of God, these no longer exist. Non-violence becomes a lived principle because the warrior sage is non-violent within. Truth becomes the reality, but it is the truth of the spiritual-Self, not the truths of religious beliefs or philosophical tenants. For the warrior sage, the only possible meaning for the term "original sin" is ignorance. Original sin is not a stain on the soul, it is ignorance of the soul. When we lose the ignorance, sin does not exist. Recall that the term ignorance means exactly what it says – to ignore, to be unconscious or unaware of. It is ignorance, lack of awareness, of the spiritual-Self as our core identity that allows us to be enslaved to the ego-self with its habits built on pain and pleasure, and its inherent fear of death, loss, and change. Sin, original and otherwise, exists only in the mind of man, not in divinity. Contrary to what religions claim, we cannot sin against God; we only sin against the beliefs of man. We cannot blaspheme God; we can only blaspheme belief systems. Remember, beliefs are not truths, they are only hypoteses of reality.

Spiritual Humanism

There is no doubt. If we examine without prejudice we see that every human being is a reservoir of great power, especially great spiritual power. Our true heritage is not fear, greed, hatred, and bigotry. We are all God in drag, and the warrior sage sleeps inside each and every one of us. We have living examples of spiritual, mental and physical power, individuals who have reached inside themselves and have become warrior sages. They are great spiritual and religious teachers, great martial artists, and great spiritual philosophers, but many also live ordinary lives, engaged in the day-to-day activities of their time and culture. Each engages the journey in his or her own way, but they all share the qualities of a spirit-centered being – universal in outlook, free of dogma, open to other ways of thought, and loving in every action they take. They are universally peaceful, loving, and wise.

Unfortunately, it is also true that only a few ever realize this power. This is somewhat puzzling as the discipline necessary to become a warrior sage is not difficult, certainly not more than any other discipline to achieve excellence in any human endeavor. No, the problem lies more in the material, ego-centric emotions and beliefs that enslave independent thought and development while driving destructive behavior.

Everywhere we look, humanity has enslaved itself to the limitations of the ego-self and materialism. In some cultures it takes the form of religion, in others politics/government, and still in others economic systems. "Enslaved" means that the power of our human spirit is bent and subservient to the limited ego-centered beliefs of the governing body politic, whether that is religious dogma, corporate policy, or government regulation. This slavery shows itself as religious intolerance and bigotry, corporate greed and economic domination, and governmental control and imperialism. All too often this is still done through brute military power. But for most, it occurs by a tyranny of the mind, accomplished through belief and the unwillingness to go beyond material form. We are constantly reminded by "authorities" that humans are limited. Science insists that material reality is all there is, and politicians proclaim that war and struggle are the only alternative.

We don't need another religion; we need to become aware of the foundation of all religions within ourselves. We don't need another belief system; we need a spiritual science with the inner technology and a practical philosophy that guides each and every one of us to our own understanding and spiritual-Self. The message of every great spiritual master, regardless of time, culture, and religious persuasion, has been that love is the only way. Christ's message was one of love, the Buddha spoke of non-harming, and Mohammed preached tolerance and charity. All the great philosophies of every major religion are based on love. So why do we find it so hard to do? It's time to wake up and really practice what the great ones taught and lived.

We must approach life with a guiding framework that incorporates a spiritual science of inner development. We must experiment rather than believe, replicate rather than blindly accept, and become skilled rather than simply informed. This framework must embrace the rich variety of religious, political, and economic expression that naturally arises from the rich variety of human experience. Within this general framework, we must engage the inner disciplines that lead to skill, and not simply let our human power develop in haphazard and incomplete ways. In short, we must have a spiritual humanism that incorporates both the science and technologies of spiritual development and expression.

In spiritual humanism, governments, economic systems, science, and religion are designed to serve man, not man designed to serve the system. In spiritual humanism, we recognize the inherent divinity of life in all its expressions, and there is respect for life rather than property. In spiritual humanism, human well-being is placed above materialism, and the purpose of business is the benefit of humanity, not profit. In spiritual humanism, science involves the subjective as a core principle, recognizing that all knowledge is a function of the subjective experience. In spiritual humanism, all religious expression is accepted as equally valid, even though not equally as sophisticated. In spiritual humanism, the life force is recognized as the primary healing agent, and healthy, whole foods, exercise, and emotional support are the primary healing agents instead of synthetic drugs and artificial means. In spiritual humanism, beliefs are tools, not truths, and dogmas are nothing more than convenient frameworks for further exploration.

The warrior sage recognizes that the core reality is divinity, and that all life is an expression of the divine. The human being is the meeting point, the integration of material nature and spiritual reality. We are spiritual-Selves, here to have human experiences, and our purpose must be to free ourselves of the fears, greed, hatreds, and violence that lock us into a living hell on earth. The Kingdom of Heaven is right before us. What do you, as the living Divinity, choose for yourself? Wake up and be the warrior sage that you are. Wake up, Ancient One, and be the love that you are.

About the Author

Phil Nuernberger, Ph.D., is a direct disciple of H.H. Swami Rama and was personally initiated and trained by him since 1970. Studying with Swamiji in the Himalayas of India and Nepal, Dr. Nuernberger is one of the few Americans to receive initiation by Swamiji into the highest levels of the tantric tradition of the Himalayan Sages. With his master's instruction and blessing, Dr. Nuernberger has been teaching and initiating others in this tradition since 1972. Beginning in 1970, he was instrumental in helping build the Himalayan Institute and served on the Board of Directors and as Senior Faculty Member until 1992. At his master's suggestion, Dr. Nuernberger also studied Washin Ryu Karate with Sensei Hidi Ochiai, a Japanese samurai, and achieved black belt ranking.

Dr. Nuernberger uniquely and skillfully combines the wisdom and knowledge of the East with the science and practicality of the West to train executives in the personal skills of strategic intelligence and leadership mastery. He has taught the integration of mind, body, and spirit and made meditation and spirituality an important part of corporate executive training for over thirty years. A pioneer in the integration of East and West, beginning in 1970, he was one of the first to:

- Develop, practice, and educate professionals in holistic health;
- Direct a successful clinical biofeedback program;
- Provide stress-management training to corporate executives;
- Introduce meditation and spirituality into executive training;
- Develop and teach an MBA course in self-mastery disciplines.

As President of Strategic Intelligence Skills, Inc., Dr. Nuernberger provides innovative programs in leadership, stress management, and personal effectiveness to executives, corporations, and business schools. His leadership in the areas of wellness, performance excellence, and practical spirituality has gained him a national and international following. Recent clients include Merrill Lynch, Securities Institute of America, J.P. Morgan Partners, and Cargill. He also serves as adjunct faculty at The Aresty Institute of Executive Education of the Wharton School of Business at the University of Pennsylvania and at DeSales University.

Dr. Nuernberger is the author of five books, including *The Warrior Sage: Life as Spirit, From Loneliness to Love* and the best-selling *Strong and Fearless: The Quest for Personal Power.*

To contact Dr. Phil Nuernberger:
Strategic Intelligence Skills, Inc.
One Rock Ledge Drive, Honesdale, PA 19431
(570) 253-4754 • www.mindmaster.com • info@mindmaster.com

Books from Yes International Publishers

Phil Nuernberger, Ph.D.
Strong and Fearless: The Quest for Personal Power
The Warrior Sage: Life as Spirit

Justin O'Brien, Ph.D.
Walking with a Himalayan Master: An American's Odyssey
Superconscious Meditation
A Meeting of Mystic Paths: Christianity and Yoga
The Wellness Tree: Dynamic Program Creating Optimal Wellness
Running and Breathing
Mirrors for Men: A Journal for Reflection

Linda Johnsen
A Thousand Suns: Designing Your Future with Vedic Astrology
The Living Goddess: Tradition of Mother of the Universe
Daughters of the Goddess: Women Saints of India
Kirtan! Chanting as a Spiritual Path (with Maggie Jacobus)

Theresa King
The Spiral Path: Explorations in Women's Spirituality
The Divine Mosaic: Women's Images of the Sacred Other

Swami Veda Bharati
Subtler than the Subtle: The Upanishad of the White Horse
The Light of Ten Thousand Suns

Prem Prakash
Three Paths of Devotion

Ron Valle and Mary Mohs
Opening to Dying and Grieving: A Sacred Journey

Rev. Alla Renee Bozarth
Soulfire: Love Poems in Black and Gold

Charles Bates
Pigs Eat Wolves: Going into Partnership with Your Dark Side

Mary Pinney Erickson and Betty Kling
Streams from the Sacred River: Women's Spiritual Wisdom

Cheryl Wall
Mirrors for Women: A Journal of Reflection

Gopala Krishna
The Yogi: Portraits of Swami Vishnu-devananda

Christin Lore Weber
Circle of Mysteries: The Women's Rosary Book

Laurie Martin
Smile Across Your Heart: The Process of Building Self Love